Search the
Scriptures

ILLUSTRATED

Search the Scriptures

ILLUSTRATED

Modern Medicine and Biblical Personages

by

ROBERT B. GREENBLATT,

M.D., C.M. (McGill), Honoris Causa (Bordeaux)
Medical College of Georgia

Foreword by
Henry King Stanford, Ph.D.

Special Illustrated Edition

BARNES & NOBLE BOOKS
TOTOWA, NEW JERSEY

Dedicated to
The students of the Medical College of Georgia
*Forty classes of whom I have been
privileged to teach, to advise, to
direct and, some of them, to inspire,
and who dedicated to me their 1960
yearbook The Aesculapian*

The College's distinguished President and past Presidents
WILLIAM H. MORETZ, M.D.
HARRY B. O'REAR, M.D.
G. LOMBARD KELLY, M.D.   EDGAR R. PUND, M.D.

*Each of them has supported the
Chair of Endocrinology*

Search The Scriptures Special Illustrated Edition
First Published in USA 1985 by
Barnes & Noble
81 Adams Drive
Totawa, New Jersey

ISBN 0-389-20545-1

Published in UK & Europe by
The Parthenon Press
Casterton Hall
Carnforth Lancs LA6 2LA

Foreword

THE BIBLE is a rich lode. Depending on what they are searching for, prospectors find a variety of nuggets in its inexhaustible seams.

Adherents of Judaism and Christianity discover deposits of divine revelation. For some it contains magnificent literature in its poetry, hymns, and dirges. For others it *is* literature, particularly the King James version, which has influenced English prose with its resonant rhythms and sonorous style. For still others it is vivid political history, narrating the ebb and flow of kingdoms in a crucial part of the world. Finally, there are those who use it as an archaeological guide to the location of many places long since obliterated by devastations from man and nature.

Now comes a distinguished endocrinologist, Robert B. Greenblatt, M.D., to do his own special kind of prospecting. Using the physician's diagnostic tools, he mines nuggets of insight into the illnesses that afflicted the Bible's storied characters. From scriptural descriptions he infers that Esau was suffering from hypoglycemia, a syndrome of low blood sugar, and thus was so deathly weak that he was willing to sell his birthright for life-sustaining "pottage." He suggests that the giant Goliath may have been suffering from a pituitary tumor, pressing on the optic nerve, which obstructed his peripheral vision and made him an easier prey for David.

Dr. Greenblatt discovers techniques that were forerunners of certain medical practices today. When the good Samaritan bound up the wounded traveller with "oil and wine," was he revealing the ingenuous conviction of the ancients that wine had curative power, explained today as the power of the benevolent fungus shared by wine and penicillin? A fascinating account of the plants and shrubs referred to as medicinals in the Bible indicates that the use of the herb aloe vera preceded by thousands of years its use today in sunburn lotions.

Anyone who has read the Bible, even in a limited way, knows of the rollicking role sex plays in the lives of its people. However, Dr. Greenblatt is the first, to my knowledge, to explain these situations from the standpoint of modern endocrinology. Did Joseph flee from his master Potiphar's wife, because of virtue or sexual inadequacy? Was Onan's form of contraception as undesirable then as now? How did the ancient city of Sodom lend its name to a description of certain sexual practices lasting down into our modern age? These questions are only a few to which Dr. Greenblatt addresses his professional expertise.

Reading the book makes me feel that I have accompanied a skillful miner deep into the Biblical deposits. I commend this exciting expedition to all who prize unusual nuggets, polished by medical fact and lively imagination.

HENRY KING STANFORD
President, University of Miami

Preface

Born of other essays written at the behest of the students at the Medical College of Georgia, and then privately published as *A Physician's Quest, Search the Scriptures* connects the human with the scientific by examining some facets of Biblical medicine under the light of present-day knowledge. It is the book not at all of a theologian, make sure, but of a physician and endocrinologist, who considers the Bible the world's greatest literary work, and who believes that the better informed we are of the past, the wiser we are in the present, and the humbler against the future.

Often in my lectures over almost a half century, I compared Biblical disorders with today's endocrinopathies, psychologic happenstances with hormonal drive, or the probable ailment of one who changed the course of history with a current illness or syndrome. These analogues fascinated my students, who were avid for knowledge of the Bible, of other classics, and of history; such parallels seemed to fill a need. "His studie was but litle on the bible" is common not alone of Chaucer's Physician, particularly as we now limit in our schools the uses of the Bible and its drama of all humanity.

The Bible (Old and New Testaments) is read for inspiration, for solace and comfort, for the beauty and power of its language. If agnostics do not regard the Scriptures as Holy Writ because of the provincialism of its ethics and mistakes of its science, they at least may agree with H. G. Wells that the Bible "is the most remarkable collection of ancient documents in the world". No other book has had so many interpreters of its every word, from the "In the beginning" of Genesis to the last "Amen" of Revelation.

The Bible, for better or worse, has been subjected over the centuries to continuous scrutiny in an effort to clarify certain phrases and perhaps correct errors in translations from the original Hebrew and Greek. The author is chagrined to find that the passage "His breasts are full of milk" (Job 21:24) which remained unchanged in the King James Version since

A.D. 1611 has been altered in the Revised Standard Version to "his body full of fat." This modification is more or less in conformity with other translations (e.g., the Latin, "His viscera are full of fat" – viscera eius plena sunt adipe; and the French, "flanks laden with fat" – les flancs chargés de graisse) and so on. How does one reconcile such tampering with Holy Writ, since it has long been believed that the Bible is inerrant, that the original text was inspired by an infallible Diety? It is reassuring to learn that the Book of Job was among the scrolls recovered from the Dead Sea caves. Written in Aramaic over 2,000 years ago, it leaves no doubts as to the meaning of the passage in question, "His teats are full of milk." Recent advances in medicine now afford a satisfactory explanation for this incredible phenomenon – lactation in the male. It is hoped that a new generation of Bible scholars will restore the original translation. Science and religion need no longer be in conflict; they can and do complement each other.

My abiding interest in the medical lore of the Bible enables me to share with you some novel interpretations which, through recent advances in the sciences, permit one to better understand certain aspects of medicine in the Bible and truths that have been overlooked or distorted. How many readers of the Bible are aware that the "gall" added to the vinegar offered to Jesus was the juice of the opium plant and not bitter bile? Many scholars maintain that the soothing potion was offered to Jesus by the Daughters of Jerusalem – a small group of Jewish women – dedicated to acts of charity and mercy. The juice of the plant called "gall" was mixed with sour wine (vinegar) not to aggravate the suffering and humiliation of those about to be crucified by the Roman soldiers but to serve as an anodyne. How many readers of the Bible are surprised to learn that "testament" derives from the fact that when an oath was sworn the hand was placed over the genitals, much as today the hand is placed on a Bible – hence, testicle, testimonial, testament?

The reception accorded the first and second editions of this book (12 and 7 printings respectively) encouraged me to add several additional chapters for a third edition (4 printings). Now comes an illustrated edition which, I hope, will continue to provide even greater pleasure to the reader, as well as furnish an insight into some medical curiosities, expose the human condition with compassion and understanding, and engender more respect for diversity than for conformity.

From *Search the Scriptures* emerges a lesser theme: the place of modern medicine and of today's physician. Recent advances in medicine, particularly in endocrinology, are wonders of the world. Only forty years ago, pneumonia was a probable, adrenal gland failure (Addison's disease) a very possible, and surgical removal of the adrenals a certain death certificate. Today, persons with pneumonia are well, often within a few days, thanks to 20 capsules of penicillin or tetracycline, and persons with Addison's disease or without their adrenals live out their lives, thanks to cortisone.

Yet the status of the physician, always the peer of priests, judges, and scholars, may be lower than it was a half-century ago. The history of medicine is the history of humanity, Garrison has observed, with "its brave aspirations after truth and finality, its pathetic failures" and perhaps the physician's place has risen and fallen with it. Perhaps too pessimistic, Job spoke of "physicians of no value" and, possibly erring with optimism, Stevenson wrote that "the physician almost as a rule" stood "above the common herd" and was, indeed, "the flower" of civilization.

It is my desire to share with the reader the joy and pleasure I have experienced in my search of the Scriptures. In this quest I am ever mindful of Alexander Pope's exhortation:

"Know then thyself, presume not God to scan,
The proper study of mankind is man."

I would express my gratitude to all who have written on Biblical medicine, though space forbids me to mention them here. But I would thank, especially, Mr. Lawrence M. Lande, for his wise counsel; Rabbi Norman Goldburg, for his frequent and pleasant help; Mrs. Martha Bell and Mrs. Karen Fischer, for their research; Mrs. Ann Hyatt, for her assistance in preparation of the manuscripts; Dr. Henry King Stanford, for the kindness of his Foreword.

ROBERT B. GREENBLATT, M.D., C.M.

Augusta, Georgia
September, 1984

Contents

CONTENTS

CONTENTS

Tamar conceals her identity from Judah.

1

The Way of a Maid With a Man

There be three things which are too wonderful for me, yea, four which I know not:

The way of an eagle in the air; the way of a serpent upon a rock; the way of a ship in the midst of the sea; and the way of a man with a maid.

Proverbs 30:18-19

Who can fathom the subtlety, the why and the wherefore, the mystifying ways of a maid with a man?

FOUR WOMEN of the Bible are worthy of our scrutiny. The first is Tamar, the crafty widow who had the courage to resolve her quest for motherhood; the second is the nameless wanton wicked woman of Proverbs, whose feet would not abide in her house as she sought her fill of love; the third is Delilah, the enchantress, who betrayed her lover for handfuls of silver; and the fourth is Mary Magdalene, the penitent sinner, who displayed a spiritual love that transcended the highest expression of physical passion.

The way of a man with a maid, despite the awe of Proverbs, is an open book. It is basic and physiologic, and wonderful for all men worthy of the name man. But the way of a maid with a man is frequently beyond comprehension. Whether born of necessity, of greed, of ambition, or of love, locked in the secret recesses of a woman's mind and body are an intuitiveness and an ingenuity that are all-pervading and that contrive to preserve the species. The trafficking in sex may take the form of subtle love, or it may serve as a means to an end.

One of the earliest sociological histories of a woman's ingenuity is recorded in Genesis, a successfully laid scheme for motherhood and marriage by Tamar, daughter-in-law of Judah. Her marriages to each of Judah's two sons ended tragically with their early deaths. One day, as Judah set off to shear his sheep, Tamar, impersonating a prostitute, settled by the wayside and awaited his passing.

When Judah saw her, he thought her to be an harlot; because she had covered her face. And he turned unto her by the way, and said, Go to, I pray thee, let me come in unto thee; (for he knew not that she was his daughter in law.) And she said, What wilt thou give me, that thou mayest come in unto me?

And he said, I will send thee a kid from the flock. And she said, Wilt thou give me a pledge, till thou send it?

And he said, What pledge shall I give thee? And she said, Thy signet, and thy bracelets, and thy staff that is in thine hand. And he gave it to her, and came in unto her, and she conceived by him.   Genesis 38:15-18

When Tamar's pregnancy became apparent after several months, she was accused of harlotry and her own father-in-law ordered her burned to death. But she presented him with his pledges—his signet, his bracelets, and his staff; and Judah, surprised, acknowledged his ownership, absolved Tamar of guilt, saying "She hath been more righteous than I," and married her. Soon afterward she gave birth to twins.

By way of a well-laid and craftily executed plan, Tamar won her man. Was this prostitution? Nay. It was a tender trap for an honored and respected personage and widower. Through levirate law, Tamar gained motherhood, a husband and the continuation of her rights. (The laws of the levirate marriage—Deuteronomy 25:5-10—provided that a brother of a deceased man should, under certain circumstances, marry the widow.) Whether this be love, physical fulfillment, or attainment of security, it matters not. It was *un fait accompli* under the laws and customs of her time. Tamar attained her goal by exploiting her resources.

For some women, sexual congress is merely a game—the chase and the kill, the satisfaction that attends the conquest of a man and his subordination to their will. They seek premarital or extramarital sexual relations not for profit but for pleasures, fancied or real. Their boredom and frustration are the root of their troubles. All too frequently, their disquietude is the product of a consuming ennui, temporarily interrupted by another adventure in sex, another conquest.

Proverbs provides us such a woman (7:9-13, 17-19):

In the twilight, in the evening, in the black and dark night:
And, behold, there met him a woman with the attire of an harlot, and subtil
of heart.
(She is loud and stubborn; her feet abide not in her house:
Now is she without, now in the streets, and lieth in wait at every corner.)
So she caught him, and kissed him, and with an impudent face said unto him
. . .

I have perfumed my bed with myrrh, aloes, and cinnamon.
Come, let us take our fill of love until the morning: Let us solace ourselves
with loves.
For the goodman is not at home, he is gone a long journey.

Across the past twenty-five centuries, this scene has not altered
much. Now, as then, many a so-called good wife searches for another
sexual experience while her husband is away. Is she a prostitute? Not
really. Yet she often is more alluring and far more dangerous than the
despised prostitute who practices her art and trade for gain. Today,
the incidence of venereal disease is rising seriously, and its rise is
caused more by promiscuity than by prostitution. The warning
sounded in Proverbs applies still. Beware! "For she hath cast down
many wounded . . ." (7:26).

Acting from quite other motives was Delilah, temptress and seducer
of the mighty Samson, whose story has inspired at least three great
works of art: Milton's epical poetic drama, *Samson Agonistes,* in 1671;
Handel's oratorio, *Samson,* in 1743; and Saint-Saens' opera, *Samson et
Dalila,* in 1877. Although a giant in strength, Samson became an easy
prey in Delilah's arms. Her tender love was a snare; while she
delighted him with her body's charms, she plotted to destroy him. For
the lords of the Philistines, in order that they might slay Samson, had
engaged her to discover the secret of his great strength. This she did,
had his hair cut off, and reduced him to a man of ordinary strength
whom her compatriots could capture and imprison—until his hair
grew again and, "eyeless in Gaza," he brought down the temple on his
enemies.

Was this prostitution? Was it not, in reality, big business, artful
manipulation, and even patriotism, possibly? Delilah's reward was
from "every one of us eleven hundred pieces of silver"—and, for a
time, peace in her country.

Thence, we come to one of the most stirring narratives in the New Testament, that of a woman who had fallen from grace and regained it. Mary of Magdala may well have suffered from a compulsion neurosis known as *nymphomania*. For was she not healed of her evil spirits and infirmities when Jesus cast out of her seven devils? Mary was a woman of rank and means; how else could she have afforded the expensive alabaster box of ointment which she brought to anoint the feet of Jesus?

And, behold, a woman in the city, which was a sinner, when she knew that Jesus sat at meat in the Pharisee's house, brought an alabaster box of (intment.

And stood at his feet behind him weeping, and began to wash his feet with tears, and did wipe them with the hairs of her head, and kissed his feet, and anointed them with the ointment. Luke 7:37-38

Mary Magdalene became His truly faithful servant, for Jesus had transformed her life. A living example of humility and unselfish devotion, she displayed a love that was triumphant, no longer sensual but spiritual. Jesus said of her: "Her sins, which are many, are forgiven; for she loved much . . ." (Luke 7:47).

Prostitutes have exemplified the essence of kindness and compassion. I am reminded of the English poet who, sick, alone, and destitute, was taken into the house of a kindly streetwalker.* He shared her bed; she fed and nurtured him back to health. Although the term Magdalene is defined by the *Concise Oxford Dictionary* as "reformed prostitute," in a world where cruelty and avarice, selfishness and hypocrisy run rampant, Magdalene has come to imply humility and lovingkindness, not a wayward woman.

The way of a man with a maid is not nearly so puzzling as the way of a maid with a man. Sexual behavior is a fabric of complexly woven threads: psychogenic, anatomic, philosophic, hormonal and state-of-health. Most men are easily aroused sexually; most women accept or reject passively. The frigid female refuses to accept a subordinate position to the stronger sex, and does not enjoy marital relations. The nymphomaniac has an insatiable sex drive; she constantly pursues gratification, however elusive and fleeting. An overwhelming sexual

*Frances Thompson had two possessions: a copy of Blake's poems and a copy of Aeschylus, and *one friend*.

4

urge in other women is the expression of either an overabundance of certain hormones, whether endogenous or exogenous, or extreme end-organ sensitivity; but nymphomania is a *psychoneurosis*, manifested by a frenetic and unreasonable sexual drive.

One must remember, as he examines the physiologic and psychologic bases of sexual behavior, that sex may be only casually related to reproduction. To pry into the modus operandi of woman's every sexual reaction, from the deeply drawn breath to the total orgasm, is fraught with obstacles; yet to understand the sexual act is not to demean ourselves, for sex colors, in some degree, our entire lives. Unlike animals, men and women employ sex to attack, to defend, to preserve; and, happily, they sublimate their sexual behavior and modify it by way of their learning, experience and culture. For most of us, it is well to remember Jesus' admonition, "He that is without sin among you, let him first cast a stone at her" (John 8:7).

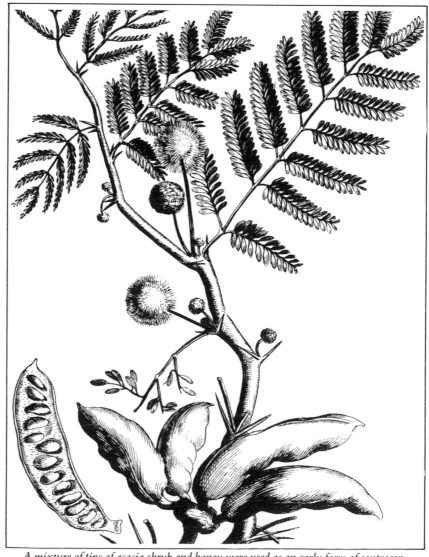

A mixture of tips of acacia shrub and honey were used as an early form of contraception.

2

Conception and Contraception

Defraud ye not one the other, except it be with consent for a time, that ye may give yourselves to fasting and prayer; and come together again, that Satan tempt you not for your incontinency.   1 Corinthians 7:5

Is temporary abstinence a satisfactory approach to contraception in love and marriage? How can man harness the "creative force" to avoid the world catastrophe of the population explosion?

A THEME in the affairs of man pervading every civilization is that conjugal love should not be hampered by fear of conception of an unwanted child. Early in Genesis (38:9), we find the story of Onan, who spilled his seed on the ground. The Bible records Tamar's widowhood and the obligation of the younger brother to marry her according to levirate law. Onan was forced to marry Tamar but wished to avoid the entanglements of paternity. Coitus interruptus, a primitive and elementary form of contraception, still is practiced widely. It is a practice that weighs on the conscience of man, and does violence to an act that should engender tenderness, fulfilment and the sublimest of emotional nuances. A great deal of illness among women, manifested in a dozen different ways, may be traced to such and other unsatisfactory sexual experiences.

Contraceptive techniques have been employed since ancient times. In the Egypt of old, a medicated tampon, prepared from a mixture of the tips of acacia shrub and honey, was inserted into the vagina. The remarkable feature of this recipe is that, under fermentation, acacia breaks down into lactic acid—one of the active spermicidal agents used today in the manufacture of contraceptive jellies. In the Dark Ages, Islamic women were advised to insert the flowers and seeds of cabbages into the vagina.

Various mechanical barriers have come into vogue from time to

7

time. Along with sheaths, diaphragms and jellies, there have been gold collar buttons for insertion into the cervical os. The lowly camel driver, aware that his transportation system might break down should one of his camels become pregnant, prevented their conceiving by inserting a pebble into the uterine cavity. In the 1920's, Berlin's Ernst Gräfenberg, transmuted the Arab camel stone into a ring of surgical silk or silver, gentle enough for the human womb. This was in preantibiotic days, and the use of the ring fell into disrepute, as much from the enmity of his professional colleagues as from corrosion, irritation and infections. But in recent years, the idea has been revised, and devices made of plastic have come into use.

The intrauterine contraceptive device, known as the IUCD or IUD, may find its greatest use in countries in which literacy is low and the population explosion dangerously high. Expulsion of the device, uterine bleeding, infection, and cramps and discomfort occur in ten to fifteen per cent of the users, and the pregnancy rates vary from one and a tenth to six per cent.

The rhythm method—that is, abstinence during the fertile period of a woman's cycle—is a method condoned, even encouraged, by the Roman Catholic Church. Not until 1930 did the Vatican modify the Augustinian rule that sex must be for procreation alone; then Pope Pius XI approved the rhythm method. A mandate for temporary abstinence, it would appear, is apparent in the Apostle Paul's Epistle to the Corinthians (7:5).

It has been conjectured that the rhythm method—discovered in this century as a method of limiting the family—was not new but merely a reaffirmation of what Paul had advised. Many years before the time of Paul, the Preacher (Ecclesiastes 3:2-5) spoke of "A time to be born, and a time to die . . . time to embrace, and a time to refrain from embracing." To read into this passage some contraceptive plan is to reach beyond the realms of reason. The rhythm method—according to Dr. Edward Tyler, an eminent authority on planned parenthood—is only seventy-five per cent effective. Because of its relatively low efficacy, many conscientious women, who have tried rhythm and failed, have given the method the sobriquet of "Roman roulette." Claire Booth Luce, a prominent Catholic, has expressed the view that the rhythm method's calculated watching is tantamount to love according to plan. Nonetheless, it is still the only technique available to millions of practicing Catholics. When in 1954 Pope Pius XII made the statement that it was the responsibility of each family not to have more children than it could take good care of, he, in effect, struck a blow for birth control. Thus he joined the responsible leaders throughout the civilized world, who realize the ominous implications of the population curve.

The modern advances in contraception are the result of newer knowledge in hormonal physiology and the science of endocrinology. The study of endocrinology has revealed the mechanisms involved in ovulation and menstruation. Now that we have discovered these secrets, and pharmaceutical laboratories have synthesized the very hormones produced by the ovary (and many other steroid preparations that simulate the action of these hormones), we can utilize our knowledge to the betterment of mankind. We have harnessed these hormones so that we can imitate the menstrual cycle; we can reproduce some of the hormonal changes that take place early in pregnancy.

Soon after conception, the ovary produces hormones to support the developing embryo and, at the same time, to prevent further ovulation, so that a woman will not conceive during her pregnancy. Nature has shown us the way, and we have applied these principles in the management of family planning. We have learned not only how to suppress ovulation but how to delay, as well as to advance, the onset of menstruation and to arrest excessive menstrual bleeding. We can help so to mold the woman of today that premenstrual tension, with all its attending unhappy situations, may be measurably lessened. We can postpone the menopause indefinitely, so that a woman in the autumn of her years need not suffer a winter of discontent. The "pill" offers women in the middle years a double blessing: through its use, the fears of childbirth are eliminated and the anxieties and depressions brought on in some women by an impending menopause are minimized.

Now there are two methods of oral contraception, the conventional "combined" form and the "sequential." Each has certain desirable features, certain advantages. At least the physician *and* the patient have choices. Furthermore, the "pill" has many uses—to regulate the cycle, to ameliorate dysmenorrhea, to prevent incapacitating ovulatory pain (*mittelschmerz*), to mitigate severe premenstrual tension, to lessen unwanted hairiness and acne in the adolescent girl, and to treat the premenopausal and menopausal woman. The "pill" is virtually 100 per cent effective when properly taken—but there are few things one

9

hundred per cent safe. Of course, complete continence is the only method one hundred per cent sure to control birth—despite the recent claims of two Englishwomen that their conceptions were parthenogenetic. A London newspaper scornfully challenged their claims. One of the offended women, claiming that her virtue and good name were sullied, brought a suit in the Courts of Law. And the Courts awarded her damages of several thousand pounds.

The ultimate goal of contraceptive measures is to provide the means whereby the destiny of man and the welfare of our world are not left to chance sexual desire alone. War, famine, poverty are the spoiled fruits of overpopulation. Hitler's *drang noch osten*, his drive to the East, was as much for *Lebensraum* for his Germans as it was for conquest. His ambition was to acquire not only living room but the wheat fields of the Ukraine to feed the increasing Teutonic masses. Even laboratory rats, packed too many in one cage, become socially maladjusted and soon will devour one another.

In 1887, when the lines of Emma Lazarus were inscribed on the pedestal of the Statue of Liberty, the population of the United States of America was about sixty million, against today's more than 200 million.

THE NEW COLOSSUS
Not like the brazen giant of Greek fame,
With conquering limbs astride from land to land;
Here at our sea-washed, sunset gates shall stand
A mighty woman with a torch, whose flame
Is the imprisoned lightning, and her name
Mother of Exiles. From her beacon-hand
Glows world-wide welcome; her mild eyes command
The air-bridged harbor that twin cities frame.
"Keep ancient lands, your storied pomp!" cries she
With silent lips. "Give me your tired, your poor.
Your huddled masses yearning to breathe free.
The wretched refuse of your teeming shore.
Send these, the homeless, tempest-tost to me,
I lift my lamp beside the golden door!"

Today the United States can no longer extend this generous offer. It must instead decrease sharply the supplies of wheat and foodstuffs to the underprivileged, overpopulated countries of the world. Our wheat bins are being rapidly emptied because of massive exports to the Soviet Union—an economic necessity to help balance the astronomic and unreasonable costs of Arab oil imports. Then, again, as our population soars, we will need the wheat to feed our own people since demographers estimate a United States population of five hundred million by 2015. Will the United States suffer the fate of India, of China?

Whether or not the church plays a constructive role in planned parenthood depends, according to sociologist Charles Hendry, on whether religious institutions are used to suppress or to release man's capacity to exercise moral responsibility. Reinhold Niebuhr believes that the function of religion is to help people develop and maintain basic faith in the meaning of life, in man's dignity, infinite worth and destiny. I have long felt that if the rhythm method is employed to circumvent conception, how can it differ morally from the pill or other contraceptive devices? The intent is the same, God is not deceived. Whatever methods are used for family spacing and limitation of the population explosion are also good for the family unit, the existing children, the health of a future child and of the mother-wife. Every child should be wanted, planned, with a design for his future welfare—not just born, like sheep or goats. All of us are born *inter fecum et urinam*; unfortunately far too many remain not far from the *feces* and the *urine*.

The mandrake root, which roughly resembled the human form, was credited with many powers to arouse ardour and to overcome barrenness.

3

Mandrake Root

And Reuben went in the days of wheat harvest, and found mandrakes in the field, and brought them unto his mother Leah. Then Rachel said to Leah, Give me, I pray thee, of thy son's mandrakes.

And she said unto her, Is it a small matter that thou hast taken my husband? and wouldest thou take away my son's mandrakes also? And Rachel said, Therefore he shall lie with thee tonight for thy son's mandrakes.

Genesis 30:14-15

Did Reuben's mandrakes have medicinal value for the promotion of fertility?

THE STORY OF JACOB'S MARRIAGE to his first cousins Rachel and Leah is a story of racial origins, of fertility and infertility, and of a bitter rivalry between two sisters.

After serving his uncle Laban for seven years, you will remember, in order to wed his younger daughter Rachel, "beautiful and well favoured," Jacob discovered himself tricked; he was wedded to the firstborn daughter Leah, the "tender eyed." So he took Rachel to wife also, promising to serve Laban "yet seven other years" for her, and loved her more than he loved Leah. Yet for a time Leah prevailed, because she could bear children. "And when the Lord saw that Leah was hated, he opened her womb": and she bore Jacob their firstborn son Reuben, him of the mandrakes, and three others, then "left bearing" until after the episode of the mandrakes.

Rachel's anguish because of her sterility bordered on the psychotic:

And when Rachel saw that she bare Jacob no children, Rachel envied her sister; and said unto Jacob, Give me children, or else I die.

And Jacob's anger was kindled against Rachel: and he said, Am I in God's stead, who hath withheld from thee the fruit of the womb?

Genesis 30:1-2

Rachel then sent her maid Bilhah to Jacob, and she bore him two sons.

13

And, countering, Leah sent her maid Zilpah to her husband, and Zilpah bore him two sons, also.

This, then, is the setting for Rachel's deal with Leah: Rachel would get Reuben's mandrakes; Leah would get the night with Jacob. Both agreed to the bargain, and it seems to have worked for both of them, for Leah now bore to Jacob two more sons and a daughter, and Rachel bore the son Joseph.

The mandrake, *Mandragora officinarum*, often miscalled Mayapple and Devil's apple, is a plant, growing in Egypt and Palestine, that is the source of a strong narcotic and of perhaps more superstitions than any other plant. Its long and twisted root, which resembles roughly the human form, was credited with many powers: to bring sleep, to kill pain, to increase wealth, to arouse ardor, to overcome barrenness. And on being uprooted, it was said to make such horrid screamings that to all who heard it came madness if not death.

Mandrakes and mandragora were known in medicine and in literature. In her dying speech, Juliet recalls the horror of the uprooted mandrakes (*Romeo and Juliet*, IV, 3):

> . . . what with loathsome smells,
> And shrieks likes mandrakes' torn out of the earth,
> That living mortals, hearing them, run mad.

In the early part of the eleventh century, Avicenna, physician-in-chief to the hospital at Bagdad, recorded in *Canon Medicinae*:

> Mandrake is the name of any natural object, for instance, a growing plant, in human shape . . . Uses and properties—It is narcotic, it exudes gum, and has juice, but the juice is stronger than the gum. Whoever wishes to have anything cut from his limbs may drink three measures of it in wine: this will produce insensibility.

In the first century, the Greek physician Dioscorides described the use of mandragora wine in surgical anesthesia and in cauterizing wounds, listed it as a bringer of sleep ("but being too much drank it drives out ye life") and, following other physicians, classified it as an aphrodisiac. Mandrakes bear a resemblance to Mexican yams, which, rich in lipids, are today the chief source of materials for the commercial synthesis of sex-steroids. Growing wild in the Holy Land in the time of Rachel and Leah, long before Dioscorides, mandragora was believed to promote fertility.

14

The *Song* of John Donne (1573–1631), the "infidel in love" and Dean of St. Paul's Cathedral in London, plays on this belief:

> Goe, and catche a falling starre
>   Get with child a mandrake roote,
> Tell me, where all past yeares are,
>   Or who cleft the Divels foot,
> Teach me to heare Mermàides singing,
> Or to keep off envies stinging,
>   And finde
>   What winde
> Serves to advance an honest minde.

But we have open to us a more plausible explanation of the role of the mandrakes in causing Rachel's fertility. From the earliest times to the most recent, a brew of the mandrake was used to quiet anxiety and to lull into rest and sleep those who sipped it. When Antony is returned to Rome in *Antony and Cleopatra* (I, 5), Cleopatra commands her servant:

> Give me to drink mandragora.
>   Why, madam?
> That I might sleep out this great gap of time
> My Antony is away.

And in *Othello* (III, 3), about to "lose" Desdemona's handkerchief in Cassio's lodging further to poison the mind of the approaching Othello, Iago gloats:

> Not poppy, nor mandragora,
> Nor all the drowsy syrups of the world
> Shall ever medicine thee to that sweet sleep
> Which thou ow'dst yesterday.

The importance of tranquility and equanimity in the management of all aspects of illness was rediscovered half a century before Shakespeare wrote about mandragora and "all the drowsy syrups of the world." Ambroise Paré (1510–1590), a volunteer field surgeon, rebelled against the redhot iron in the treatment of battle wounds. He appreciated calming influences for his patients—to quiet nerves, to promote sleep and to alleviate pain. He thought he had not only to cure but to comfort the sick, the wounded and the dying. Called to

Flanders to treat the Duke d'Auret, who had suffered for months from a gunshot wound, Paré emphasized the importance of environment, of equanimity, and of repose in treatment. He had flowers placed in the Duke's sickroom, induced his sleep by simulated rain—"by making water run from some high place into a cauldron"—and, to lift his patient's spirits, had violins played at his bedside. Small wonder that this lowly barber-surgeon ultimately became the sixteenth century's greatest surgeon. An aphorism credited to Paré succinctly sums up his philosophy toward the sick,

Quérir parfois,
Soulager souvent,
Consoler tousfois. *

What role did the mandrakes play in overcoming Rachel's infertility, and perhaps Leah's also? What helped Rachel to conceive was not the fertilizing but the tranquilizing properties of the mandrake; the mandrakes soothed her anxieties and diminished the self-reproach that she suffered because of her barrenness.

The use of tranquilizers in the management of barren but otherwise healthy couples was tested in a carefully controlled experiment. Dr. Lawrence Banks and his colleagues treated thirty women, classified as "no reason for infertility," and with daily doses of tranquilizer for three months. If conception did not occur during this period, the wife was continued on the medication *with her husband*: when both husband and wife were treated, pregnancy was fifty per cent greater. Far too long has the need to soothe anxieties and to eliminate self-reproach of both the wife and the husband been neglected in the treatment of infertility. Success may be achieved often—to "get with child a mandrake root."

*To cure, sometimes; to alleviate, often; to comfort, always.

16

The meeting of Esau and Jacob – the Bible's most famous twins.

18

4

Behold, There Were Twins

And when her days to be delivered were fulfilled, behold, there were twins
in her womb.   Genesis 25:24

*Can the tools of science be used today to foil the
laws of nature and of genetics, and to induce
multiple births?*

THE GENETIC PHENOMENON of multiple births is not yet
fully understood, and many argue the relative importance of
heredity and environment. A role of environment in biology was
furnished us by Jacob's contractual arrangement with his father-in-
law, Laban. After removing all the speckled and spotted cattle from
Laban's herds, Jacob was to receive all those that were born with these
very same genetic characteristics. Accordingly, Jacob exposed striped
rods to the constant view of the animals: "And the flocks conceived
before the rods, and brought forth cattle ringstraked, speckled, and
spotted" (Genesis 30:39).

Shakespeare used this episode, one may recall, as several kinds of
background in *The Merchant of Venice* (I, 3):

> *Shylock.* When Jacob graz'd his uncle Laban's sheep—
> This Jacob from our holy Abram was. . . .
> *Antonio.* And what of him? Did he take interest?
> *Shy.* No, not take int'rest, not, as you would say,
> Directly int'rest. Mark what Jacob did. . . .
> This was a way to thrive, and he was blest;
> And thrift is blessing, if men steal it not.

Twins are mentioned but three times in the Bible, twice in the Old
Testament and once in the New. The Bible's famous twins were Jacob
and Esau (Genesis 25:24–26). The others were Pharez and Zarah
(Genesis 38:27–30), the offspring of Tamar, who enticed her father-in-

19

law, Judah, into a levirate marriage. The only twin mentioned in the New Testament is the Apostle Thomas, called Didymus (John 20:24); the Greek word for twin is *didymus*. In Acts 28:11, Paul obliquely refers to twins when he mentions that he had wintered in the isle whose sign was Castor and Pollux. The ancient Greeks wove many legends about the gigantic twins, Castor and Polydeuces (the latter called Pollux by the Romans), offspring of Leda's amours with her mortal husband and the god Zeus.

Multiple siblings, regarded by many primitive people as evil spirits, were generally put to death. But other societies considered twins as a sign of favor from the fertility gods. Twins were honored as possessors of supernatural powers. Romulus and Remus, according to Roman legend, were twins nurtured by a wolf, who founded Rome.

The strong and sometimes psychic attachment of twins and more often their bitter rivalry have been dealt with in drama and fiction. The rivalry between Jacob and Esau is well known. The Bible states "and the children struggled together within her" (Genesis 25:22), probably representing the earliest reference on record of sibling rivalry. In the case of Pharez and Zarah, there was the struggle for emergence.

And it came to pass, when she travailed, that the one put out his hand: and the midwife took and bound upon his hand a scarlet thread, saying, This came out first.

And it came to pass, as he drew back his hand, that, behold, his brother came out: and she said, How hast thou broken forth? this breach be upon thee: therefore his name was called Pharez.

And afterwards came out his brother, that had the scarlet thread on his hand: and his name was called Zarah. (Genesis 38:28-30)

In countries today in which the right of primogeniture is observed, the claim of the firstborn to the father's title or estate could have enormous significance. Among the royal families in Europe, should twins be born, the right to succession could be in dispute unless the firstborn is officially identified. When twins are fathered by a king of the Kuanyama of South Africa, one of the babies is killed by the midwives. Dumas played upon the theme of the twin problem in his novel, *The Vicomte de Bragelonne*. He made use of the legend that France's "Man in the Iron Mask" was actually the twin brother of Louis XIV, whom the King sought to keep out of the way.

Human twins are born once in every 80 pregnancies, triplets once in 6,400, quadruplets once in 512,000, quintuplets once in about 41 million. But new fertility agents have wrought havoc with such statistics The incidence of multiple births in women treated with these agents has increased tenfold. These agents are Clomid, a pituitary gonadoptropic releasing agent; Pergonal, an extract from the urine of menopausal women rich in human pituitary gonadotropins, and gonadotropins, extracted from human pituitary glands.

Incidentally, the Pergonal available in today's pharmaceutical market is derived from a process developed by Dr. Pietro Donini of Rome; the source of its menopausal urine is a nunnery housing aged nuns. The first clinical trials with this "extract" were performed by Dr. Bruno Lunenfeld in Israel. Pergonal is doubly blessed, bearing the stamp of both Rome and the Holy Land.

Most investigators believe that monozygotic twinning (identical twins) is not hereditary, and that it occurs randomly, at any time, at any age, and in any population. Dizogotic twinning (fraternal or unidentical twins) occurs so frequently in some families that geneticists are certain the tendency is inherited, decreases in frequency from North to South, and is extremely rare in some populations. Some forty years ago, a Frenchwoman living in Cleveland, Ohio, gave birth as follows: with her first husband, twins; with her second husband, twins and triplets; with the third, twins, triplets and quadruplets. In fifteen pregnancies, she bore forty-two children, of whom twenty were stillborn, six died young, and sixteen survived. In recent years, there has been a rash of reports of quadruplets and quintuplets born to women after the administration of fertility-inducing agents and sometimes some months after terminating a course of birth control pills (this latter phenomenon has not been substantiated statistically). Dr. Carl Gemzell, of Stockholm, Sweden—noted for the treatment of infertile women with gonadoptropic extracts from human pituitaries—reported the birth of twins, triplets, quadruplets, quintuplets and sextuplets in his series. Man's upper limit seems to be sextuplets, although there have been recent reports of septuplets and octuplets. A sixteenth century memorial plaque in Germany tells of the births of seven living infants, the last of whom survived eleven days, but the story's veracity is doubtful. Not to be doubted, however, is the birth of septuplets to a Boston woman, twenty-three years old, at St. Margaret's Hospital on October 1, 1966. The three boys and four

21

girls were born four months prematurely and, therefore, never really had a chance to survive. The husband, a garbage collector, gained brief immortality; actually, no prowess belonged to him, for his wife had been treated with one of the fertility-inducing agents.

With a better understanding of the use of fertility agents, the incidence of multiple births in excess of twinning may be greatly reduced. Dr. A. Carl Crooke, of Birmingham, England, uses human gonadotropins in a single massive dose instead of daily doses over a period of eight days or more. The incidence of multiple births in his cases has decreased considerably in comparison to that of his colleagues. With the use of Clomid, the nonsteroidal pill that stimulates the release of the patient's own gonadotropins, many multiple births have been reported. From the 1,450 pregnancies on record following the administration of Clomid, two sets of quintuplets have resulted, six sets of quadruplets, eight sets of triplets, and 113 sets of twins. At the Medical College of Georgia, where the use of Clomid for the treatment of the anovulatory infertile women originated, eight sets of twins have been born out of a total of eighty-six deliveries. One set was monozygotic and must be considered a random event; the other seven sets were dizygotic due to multiple ovulations. All but one set survived; they remain well and apparently in good heath. With lowered dosages of Clomid, it may well be that the incidence of triplets and quadruplets and other multiple births may be kept in check. Our series of conceptions following Clomid continues to grow into the hundreds. The incidence of twinning remains about the same; triplets and quadruplets have not been encountered. A newly discovered fertility drug, a derivative of ergot was developed by the Swiss pharmaceutical firm of Sandoz (E. Fluekeger, and H. R. Wagner, 1968). Lutterbeck, Pryor, Varga and Wenner reported (1971) that brom-ergo-cryptine suppresses abnormal lactation. This agent was found effective in overcoming infertility in many amenorrheic women particularly in those suffering from persistent lactation (amenorrhea-galactorrhea syndromes).

Science has reached the point at which it can create a physiologic environment to increase the chances of multiple births and thus to make hereditary and genetic factors secondary. What is most awesome is the power over life and death now residing in the physician-scientist because of the great advances in human biology.

22

David and Goliath.

24

5

Giants in Those Days

And there went out a champion, out of the camp of the Philistines, named Goliath, of Gath, whose height was six cubits and a span.

And he had an helmet of brass upon his head, and he was armed with a coat of mail; and the weight of the coat was five thousand shekels of brass. . . .

And the Philistine said, I defy the armies of Israel this day; give me a man, that we may fight together. . . .

And David said to Saul, Let no man's heart fail because of him; thy servant will go and fight with this Philistine. . . .

So David prevailed over the Philistine with a sling and with a stone, and smote the Philistine, and slew him; but there was no sword in the hand of David. *Samuel 17:4-5, 10, 32, 50*

> *How could an unarmed youth dare battle the well-armored giant, Goliath? What permitted him to accept the challenge—bravado, faith, or knowledge born of clinical observation?*

THE PROWESS of giants is legend. Their conquest by men of normal proportion is celebrated in song and story. Consider the tale of Hercules' triumph over Antaeus, son of Terra, invincible so long as his feet touched the earth. Children delight in the age-old tale of *Jack and the Beanstalk*, simply because a boy was able to best a giant. Yet the story of Goliath and David holds deeper meaning and appeals to young and old. The giant Goliath, whom the Bible records as being ten feet tall, was slain by the courageous shepherd lad, David, after swaggering about for forty days to taunt the Israelites in battle array. He challenged them to send forth their champion whom he would engage in mortal combat, to decide whether the Philistines or the Israelites were the victors.

Goliath was a fearful figure, who shouted defiance and hurled insults at the enemy. Then the youthful David arrived on the field, with food and a message that his father wished delivered to his older sons. David could observe closely the boastful, threatening giant who failed to impress him. Being both perceptive and courageous, David soon requested King Saul's permission to accept Goliath's challenge. When the king was unable to dissuade him, he offered the youth full battle regalia, but David decided to face his foe unencumbered.

> And he took his staff in his hand, and chose him five smooth stones out of the brook. . . ; and his sling was in his hand: and he drew near to the Philistine.   1 Samuel 17:40

Discovering his young opponent, Goliath cursed him, enraged that an untrained boy was chosen to represent the Israelites. He swore to make quick shrift of the matter.

Did David's boldness border on youthful irresponsibility and impulsiveness? It is far more likely that his keen powers of observation disclosed Goliath's peculiar movements. David probably realized that his opponent was forced to turn his entire head in order to focus his full gaze on an object. Also, he probably found significance in the fact that such a man needed to be heavily armored and used the services of a smaller Philistine to carry a coat of mail to give additional protection. In modern terms, one might say that he suspected the loud-mouthed giant of being "all bark and no bite."

Perhaps David suspected what we know today: giants are prone to suffer from lateral blindness. Giantism is frequently caused by a tumor of the pituitary gland. As such tumors enlarge, they encroach on the inner fibers of the optic nerves and thus compromise the nerve supply to the retina. When this occurs, the victim suffers from "tunnel vision." His sight is clear in a direct line, but not peripherally. David, therefore, would step agilely to the side when he had drawn close enough to Goliath. Then, as his adversary hesitated, clumsily turning his head to bring back the youth within his limited field of vision,* David, undoubtedly skilled in the art of slinging, took deadly aim with the slingshot and struck the lone spot unprotected by heavy armor. The blow on his forehead spelled defeat for the giant. Thus David won his victory by superior knowledge, skill, and agility, rather than by brute force.

Giants have intrigued mankind since the dawn of history. Yet little

---

*"And the Philistine came on and drew near unto David. . . . and . . . the Philistine *looked about*, and saw David. . . ." (1 Samuel 17:41-42).

was known of them until late in the nineteenth century, when an interrelationship was established between the pituitary gland and a type of giantism known as *acromegaly*. Pierre Marie's classic description of this filled a page in the early annals of endocrinology, directing attention to the pituitary gland as a regulator of growth. Subsequently, it was demonstrated that acidophilic cell tumors of the pituitary are often associated with *acromegaly* and *acromegalic giantism*. In ancient days, giants often were regarded as semigods. Genesis records:

> There were giants in the earth in those days; and also after that, when the sons of God came in unto the daughters of men, and they bare children to them, the same became mighty men which were of old, men of renown.
>
> Genesis 6:4

The biblical scribe also referred to giants encountered by the Israelites as they made their way to the Promised Land. We read of the King of Bashan whose name was Og, and it is stated that his bedstead was made of iron. To portray his size, it was written that this measured nine cubits in length and was four cubits wide. He was mentioned as being the only remaining giant (Deuteronomy 3:11). Among the most graphic descriptions, however, were those spoken by the men sent by Moses to look over the Land of Canaan before it was claimed by the Israelites. They reported that although the land flowed "with milk and honey," they dared not invade it because the inhabitants were giants "and we were in our own sight as grasshoppers, and so we were in their sight" (Numbers 13:33). Yet at a later time, Joshua led them in conquering this land.

Despite such accounts, the question remains: Did actual giants inhabit the earth in the remote past? Did men with giant-sized proportions live during a prehistoric period? Of course, dinosaurs and gigantic beasts roamed the earth then. Their skeletons and lifelike replicas are exhibited by such museums as The Smithsonian Institution. However, anthropologic discoveries have yet to provide evidence that human giants have ever existed.

But we know now that excessive stature falls into three categories: the first is caused by an increased secretion of growth hormone from the pituitary gland; the second is hereditary, due to genetic factors; and the third results from continued linear growth when inactive gonadal hormones fail to stimulate closure of the epiphyses, the growing end of bones, and such victims are known as eunuchoidal giants. This third type, the eunuchoid, is generally beardless, weak, shy, nonaggressive, and his muscle mass is poor—the opposite of tall, agile, well-coordinated, and virile men of basketball fame, whose statures are the products of genetics and good nutrition. This latter type, found in certain areas of the world, includes the Watusis and Dinkas of Africa. Members of these tribes are famed for their excellent physiques: it is not unusual for them to exceed seven feet in height.

The height of young girls is increasing considerably. We now see adolescent girls who are sixty-six to sixty-nine inches in height, with a potential of seventy-two inches and more. For those destined to be extremely tall, much may be done to curtail and limit the growth spurt that occurs between eleven and thirteen years of age.

The administration of large continuous doses of estrogens (the female hormone) for six to eighteen months, and the induction of menses with small courses of progestogen administered at monthly intervals, will hasten closure of the growing ends of the bones (epiphyses), so that the girls will reach a height of two to four inches less than that predicted by growth tables. It is now possible to mitigate the economic, psychological, and physical handicaps associated with excessive tallness in girls.

We are aware that an occasional circus freak is afflicted with pituitary giantism. Yet well-known personalities of our time may also have had this disorder. Primo Carnera, that towering prize fighter of the 1930's, had definite acromegalic features. The most unforgettable, however, was Luis Firpo, who in 1923 challenged Jack Dempsey for the world's heavyweight boxing title. To everyone's astonishment, he knocked Dempsey through the ropes during the first round. Yet the champion regained his poise and remained confident. He had discovered that it was necessary to discard his usual confrontation. Instead, he adopted tactics of circling and crouching, which presented his only hope of triumphing over the towering and formidable Firpo. One may now ask whether his opponent was hampered by some degree of tunnel vision. The champion, it appeared, allowed him wide berth, carefully staying within the blurred fringes of his sight.

The lesson taught by David is a simple one: no man should be daunted by seemingly immeasurable odds or encumbered by man-made rules. Greatness is hardly ever the product of conformity, overprotectiveness and security. Life's best armaments are courage and the will to achieve. When we consider thoughtfully the way in which a youthful shepherd boy slew a giant before whom an army trembled, we cannot ignore the lesson. By persevering, man can find a way ultimately to overcome any handicap; more important than size are those barriers formed by heredity and environment, especially position. David's triumph over Goliath provides a basis for understanding the meaning, which seems a paradox of the epigram: "the race is not to the swift, nor the battle to the strong . . . but time and chance happeneth to them all" (Ecclesiastes 9:11).

Zacchaeus viewing Jesus from a sycomore tree.

6

Great of Will – Small of Stature

And, behold, there was a man named Zacchaeus, which was the chief among the publicans, and he was rich.

And he sought to see Jesus who he was; and could not for the press, because he was little of stature.

And he ran before, and climbed up into a sycomore tree to see him: for he was to pass that way.　　　　　　　　　　　　　　　　Luke 19:2-4

> *Are small men more materialistic, pragmatic, successful than large men? If so, is theirs a mechanism to compensate for what they feel is adversity?*

DO MEN SMALL OF STATURE drive to a station of success far earlier and possibly more frequently than others? Is their achievement the result of an inner drive that is physiologic; that is, tempered by *androgenic* activity? Or is it psychologic: that is, a compensatory mechanism?

In a few sentences, Luke the Physician gives us the image of a successful man of small stature and admits us into his character. Bent on seeing Jesus, Zaccheus overcame his handicap of size with characteristic determination and resourcefulness.

And when Jesus came to the place, he looked up, and saw him, and said unto him, Zacchaeus, make haste, and come down: for today I must abide at thy house.　　　　　　　　　　　　　　　　Luke 19:5

Jesus had come to Jericho on His ministry—only now to become the guest of a sinner, the principal tax collector, the man most despised in the city.

Zaccheus displayed unusual agility and strength in climbing the sycomore tree. He was in the right place, at the right time, and even

31

with the right words: "Behold, Lord, the half of my goods I give to the poor; and if I have taken any thing from any man by false accusation, I restore him fourfold." To which Jesus replied: "This day is salvation come to this house" (Luke 19:8-9). Zaccheus had won the honors: he was a natural winner, even to the measure that Jesus permitted him to keep half of his worldly possessions.

Legend clothes the accomplishments of men of small stature. Court jesters were often dwarfs; their entree permitted them to influence and advise rulers. Many became privy counselors. Attila, King of the Huns and "the Scourge of God"—short, with large head, snub nose, broad chest and deep-set eyes—was quite likely an *achondroplastic* dwarf; aggressive and ruthless, he overran Europe and knocked at the gates of Rome. Toulouse-Lautrec, the French painter, suffered from *osteogenesis imperfecta*; during his youth, his brittle bones were fractured so often that he grew up deformed, small, and twisted—a pathetic caricature of a man. Yet he would not be denied fame and success.

Strutting Mussolini and vainglorious Hitler were men of diminutive height who positioned themselves at the council tables on levels higher than those about them. Their fatuous concern about size is reminiscent of Philip III of Spain. Philip harbored such a deep inferiority complex that he insisted that all who addressed him do so on their knees, for he was very short, and practically everyone with whom he had contact, courtier or peasant, towered over him. It is of some interest to observe also that Spain's Franco was less than five feet tall.

Napoleon Bonaparte is, of course, the classic example of the undersized aggressive man. Forcing circumstances to favor him, "le petit caporal" rose fast: a general at twenty-four and the Emperor at thirty-five, he sought to conquer all of Europe, often in the name of freedom. For a time Beethoven was taken in by Napoleon, and placed his name as Pro Consul on the title page of his Third Symphony, the great *Eroica*. But when Napoleon declared himself Emperor, Beethoven struck it off in grand anger.

Whether a success or a failure, saint or tyrant, every person is the product of his environment—a frequent theme of poets. Lord Byron's Childe Harold, for example, says: "I live not in myself, but I become/Portion of that around me. . . ." And when the aged Ulysses, leaving to his son Telemachus his scepter and his isle, begins his last voyage—"To sail beyond the sunset, and the baths / Of all the western stars, until I die"—Tennyson has him say:

I am a part of all that I have met;
Yet all experience is an arch wherethro'
Gleams that untravell'd world, whose margin fades
Forever and forever when I move.

But every person is also the product of his heredity, as well as of his nutrition and of endemic disease; these play important roles in the molding of men, of nations, and of civilizations. Surely he is the product of the activity of his endocrine glands, for in every person they affect every cell: they influence mental acuity, physical agility, build and stature, growth of body hair and pitch of voice, sexual urges and total behavior. His endocrine system tempers man's every moment.

Not all men small of stature are resourceful and successful, of course. Nor are individuals short because of genetic and nutritional reasons alone; many are so because of a precocious output of testicular hormones—the androgens. These hasten the closure of the growing ends of bones, the epiphyses, and thus prevent further growth in stature. Small men are usually strong, agile, and aggressive—qualities that manifest good androgenic function. Maturing earlier than their fellows, yet seeing themselves as handicapped, they grasp for attainments; the taste of petty victories whets their appetites for more, nothing succeeding like success. Their triumphs spur further accomplishments and begin a process that continues throughout their lives.

Excessive tallness—when the result of good nutrition, good health, and good hereditary traits—may have its discomfitures and inconveniences, but withal many advantages, too. Tall men, when favored with a personality to harmonize with their stature, frequently become leaders of men. On the other hand, many tall men are tall because of delayed testicular activity; their full measure of growth occurs before the complete impact of testicular androgens is felt. In fact, tallness that is excessive is not infrequently a feature of the eunuchoid, who has congenitally poor androgenic or testicular function. As a result, such a man is meek and suppliant, shy and retiring, wanting force and fight.

The story of Saul, the first king of all the Jews, contrasts with that of Zaccheus. Whereas Zaccheus was "little of stature," Saul stood head and shoulders taller than the rest, and he was handsome: "there was not among the children of Israel a goodlier person" (1 Samuel 8:2) Yet when he was to be presented to the gathered throngs, he hid. Eventually found, he managed to stand before the people and to hear their shout: "God save the king!" (10:24)—a salute which has echoed down the ages. Although King Saul was not eunuchoid, his meekness, shyness, and inordinate humility were not manly qualities, surely, and one may conjecture about the measure of his androgenic function and of his virility. At any rate, Saul proved a weak king and a failure, subject to intense and disabling psychic conflicts that at last destroyed him.

Men of diminutive stature often have a compelling desire to compensate for their slightness of build by excelling in their tasks. Their drive to succeed is the by-product of heritable traits, environmental influences such as state of health and, not the least, endocrinal function.

Whereas love and charity, pity, compassion and kindly consideration are said to derive from the influences exerted by the female sex hormones common to both men and women, qualities of ambition, drive, valor, aggressiveness, militant truculence and bravado, cocksureness and acquisitiveness are said to derive from the male sex hormones. During puberty, excessive endogenous androgens will induce early sexual maturation, vigor and strength, and early closure of the growing bone ends, the epiphyses. Many short persons have the strength and the will to overcome their imagined handicap of stature.

Zaccheus, the impudent tax collector, was in the employ of the hated Roman conquerors to "render unto Caesar the things that are Caesar's." In his endeavor for wealth and power, he placed self-interest above the respect of his own people; rich and ambitious, he was known as a selfish opportunist. Was it curiosity or need which drove Zaccheus to seek Jesus? Whichever the case, Zaccheus appears to have done an about-face after his confrontation with Jesus. Luke, certainly, considered this man's attributes worth recording in his Gospel.

Joseph being sold by his brothers into Egyptian slavery.

7

Righteous Indignation

And she caught him by his garment, saying, Lie with me: and he left his
garment in her hand, and fled, and got him out.   Genesis 39:12

*Joseph fled from the bedchamber of Potiphar his
master's wife for what reason? Was it his virtue
alone? Or something else?*

JOSEPH WAS A GOODLY MAN and "well favoured" when he
served his Egyptian master, Potiphar, as overseer of his house, of
his fields, and of all his possessions. In the routines of his business, he
was exposed daily to the wiles of his master's wife, a particularly
aggressive temptress. Day after day she sought to entice him, but "he
hearkened not unto her, to lie by her, or to be with her." And when
one day she caught him by his garment, he fled, probably in panic,
leaving his garment in her hand.

Was Joseph motivated by his code of ethical behavior or, one may
speculate, by fear of his sexual inadequacy? His history we may
appreciate fully only if we view it from several perspectives. It is a
story of morality and of triumph over adversity, but even more, a
story filled with significance for the endocrinologist. Almost certainly,
Joseph suffered from delayed *pubescence* together with the pangs and
torments associated with retarded physical and sexual development.
Deep were his emotional turmoil, his insecurity, his envy of the
virility of his brothers, and the psychosexual trauma that ensued.

An impotent man disregards temptations of the flesh more easily
than a potent man. As a beautiful woman maintains her virtue with
greater difficulty than an unsightly one, so a virile man must show
greater restraint than one less virile. A philosopher held that "only he
is virtuous who, having known both good and evil, chooses the good."
By this standard, Joseph was not a virtuous man: he had not known evil
as applied to carnal knowledge. He was an innocent young man in his

37

twenties, completely lacking in experience of the way of a man with a maid.

Faced with the seductive charms of Potiphar's wife, was he unequal to the task? A young man with a clinical history of retarded sexual development naturally fears the advances of a beguiling female. Joseph could not and would not submit to the lust-thirsty wife of Potiphar, and he fled from her chamber. "Hell hath no fury like a woman scorned:" Joseph was soon adjudged a would-be rapist, and for the judgment spent three years in jail.

What evidence can we adduce that Joseph suffered from delayed pubescence and sexual inadequacy? Many of his traits indicate immaturity. Although seventeen years old, Joseph tattled on his brothers by bringing "their evil report" to Jacob, his father. He was gentle, effeminate, and handsome in a girlish way. Jacob, a man of deep insight, sought to compensate for his son's frailties by openly lavishing love and attention to him—this child of his life's twilight. Befittingly, the father made for him a "coat of many colours." The situation was one to arouse tension, and Joseph exacerbated it further by telling his dreams with special arrogance—and revelation.

A Freudian interpretation of the first of his dreams suggests clearly that he was a sexually retarded boy:

> Hear, I pray you, this dream which I have dreamed:
> For, behold, we were binding sheaves in the field, and, lo, my sheaf arose, and also stood upright; and, behold, your sheaves stood round about, and made obeisance to my sheaf. Genesis 37:6-7

In his fantasy, Joseph found fulfillment of his wish, his craving for the attainment of manhood and of sexual potency. His longing for sexual prowess was father to the thought symbolically expressed in his dream.

His words so provoked the older brothers that they determined to be rid of him. Only the remorse of the eldest, Reuben, who still referred to the seventeen-year-old Joseph as "the child," prevented them, in Dothan, from murdering him. Instead, they sold him for twenty pieces of silver to a group of traveling Ishmaelites, who brought him to Egypt, and sold him to Potiphar, captain of Pharaoh's guard (Genesis 37:27-36).

Prison life provided Joseph with valuable time for study, contemplation and self-inventory; there he hardened and matured. Because of his ability to interpret dreams, he was called before the Pharaoh to explain the ruler's dreams of the seven lean and the seven fat kine. Joseph predicted that seven years of plenty would be followed by seven years of famine. Pharaoh was so impressed that he rewarded him by making him the overlord of Egypt, a position of great responsibility for one but thirty years of age. Joseph grew in power and in stature. True to his prediction, plenty was followed by famine, for which he had prepared the nation. In the meantime, he wed the daughter of one of the high priests, and she bore him two sons.

During the long famine, which also scourged Canaan, Joseph's brothers came to Egypt to buy corn. He recognized them but they did not know him, for he was now fully a man, an attainment that they could not have foreseen. Remembering his dreams of them, he twice taunted them with a meaningful reminder of his earlier handicap: "Ye are spies; to see the nakedness of the land ye are come." The repetition of "nakedness," synonym and symbol for genital exposure, is significant. Finally, Joseph revealed his identity, tearfully kissed his brothers, and brought about a reconciliation of his entire family.

Sexual immaturity, often equated with delayed pubescence rather than with a true disorder of the endocrine glands, is accompanied by mental and emotional anguish. For some, the psychic scars are erased, given time, as maturation comes. For others, their trauma, indelibly inscribed on their personalities, is forever reflected in their behavior. Secondary sex characteristics fail to develop in those with *pituitary gland* or *testicular* deficiencies. Unless substitutional hormone therapy is prescribed, the unmistakable evidence of their disorder persists throughout their lives.

Today, much may be done to promote sexual maturation. Androgens, the so-called male sex hormones, can stimulate earlier development of secondary sex characteristics, and thus circumvent the possibility of irreversible personality defects. There are those, however, who feel that nature must be allowed to take its course—and its toll. The story of Joseph provides much food for thought; it is, in part, a clinical drama of delayed pubescence.

THE EUNOCH AND PHILLIP

St. Phillip and the eunuch.

40

8

And They Sang Like Cherubs

For there are some eunuchs, which were so born from their mother's womb: and there are some eunuchs, which were made eunuchs of men: and there be eunuchs, which have made themselves eunuchs for the kingdom of heaven's sake. He that is able to receive it, let him receive it.

Matthew 19:12

Why emasculation? What is the role of the endocrine glands in the development of character and personality?

FROM REMOTE ANTIQUITY, eunuchs were employed among the Orientals to take charge of their women, and among the Greeks to serve as their chamberlains. The practice of castrating boys to be sold as eunuchs for Moslem harems continued into modern times. Thus, physical changes wrought by emasculation in both man and beast have been known from the earliest period in our civilization.

What is more remarkable, however, is that two-thousand years ago Jesus pointed out that "some eunuchs . . . were so born from their mother's womb." Long before the science of endocrinology became a discipline in medicine, we have recorded for us a diagnosis of congenital *eunuchoidism* or primary testicular failure.

The hormones produced by the male and female gonads have been called sex hormones because they are responsible for the development of secondary sex characteristics. However, their effects on the human organism are many, in addition to their influence on maleness or femaleness. They regulate certain aspects of metabolism, such as conservation of proteins and modification of calcium utilization, as well as affect the molding of character and personality. Eunuchs castrated in boyhood are known for their fidelity; those castrated later in life often have been suspect, correctly.

Although centuries may have elapsed before primitive people

41

realized the relationship between sexual intercourse and the miracle of reproduction, sketches of sexual organs drawn on the walls of caves inhabited by prehistoric man attest that from the earliest times man has been fascinated by sex. The excavated walls of Pompeii and the statues adorning the temples of ancient India reveal ornamental drawings of the sex act. A bas-relief of Assyrian origin, dating back many centuries before the Christian Era, depicts a vizier and a eunuch, in which the contrast between a normal and a mutilated male is vividly portrayed. All this and the frequent references in the Bible to matters sexual testify to an appreciation of the role of sex in the daily life of man.

Replacement therapy that substitutes purified hormones for glandular deficiencies occupies an important place in the therapeutic armamentarium of today's endocrinologist. Yet the science of organotherapy had early beginnings: primitive man had notions similar to those of the modern endocrinologist, although he employed them in a vastly different fashion. He attributed great virtue to the internal organs obtained from slain enemies or from animals; the ancient warrior sought to increase his courage by eating the heart of his adversary, or to heighten his sexual power by partaking of his enemy's testicles.

For several hundred years, it was common practice to treat diseases of certain organs with like tissues from healthy animals. In fact, the first successful endocrine preparation was whole thyroid gland— served fried—for the treatment of thyroid deficiency. It is not surprising, therefore, that as late as 1889 the famous Charles-Edouard Brown-Sequard (1817-1894), son of an American father and a French mother and successor of Claude Bernard as professor of experimental medicine at the Collège de France, treated himself for waning vigor with injections of pasteurized water extracts prepared from dogs' testicles. At the age of seventy-two, this hoary-headed scientist reported his own spectacular rejuvenation before the Société de Biologie de Paris. He captured the imagination of the medical world, and his new form of therapy caught on with contagious enthusiasm.

Neither Brown-Sequard nor his students realized, however, that the testes and ovaries are unlike the thyroid in that they do not store hormones in any quantity but, instead, rapidly secrete them into the bloodstream. To furnish the average dose of *testosterone*, the male sex hormone employed as a therapeutic measure, would require about one-quarter ton of bulls' testes. Testosterone is synthesized in the laboratory in a pure form identical to that produced by the testes. The "good results" experienced by Brown-Sequard and thousands of other gullible males were due entirely to autosuggestion. Worthless desiccated orchid substance (tablets of dried testicular powder) were marketed for many years before endocrinology came of age some three or four decades ago, having received a great impetus from the work of Brown-Sequard.

Although endocrine therapy was conceived in error, owing to subjective interpretation, it nevertheless, opened the way for future generations to improve and perfect. Today the eunuchoid male need not be the object of such curiosity as the beardless and goat-voiced Pardoner was in the Prologue of Chaucer's *Canterbury Tales*:

> Swiche glaringe eyen hadde he as an hare,
> A vernicle hadde he sowed on his cappe.
> His walet lay biforn him in his lappe,
> Bret-ful of pardoun come from Rome al hoot.
> A voys he hadde as smal as hath a goot.
> Ne berd hadde he, ne never sholde have,
> As smothe it was as it were late y-shave;
> I trowe he were a gelding or a mare.

Today the Pardoner's condition may be remedied. The high-pitched voice, the scanty or absent beard, the poor muscular development, the lack of sexual drive, and the smallness of the *phallus*—these endocrinology may stimulate toward normalcy by vigorous treatment with pure synthetic testosterone or its analogues.

Matthew reports that Jesus spoke of eunuchs "which were made eunuchs of men." Actually, castration was practiced for centuries before the Christian Era, but it was practiced particularly on common farm animals in order to tame them and make them more useful for work. What was not understood was that this form of mutilation, for the best results, must be performed before maturity in both man and beast.

Castration performed on a boy results in the complete failure of development of his secondary sex characteristics; this developed the type of eunuch who was employed as the highly specialized watchman, as the guardian of the couch or the harem guard. However, if castration is performed after maturity, regressive changes of various degree, as well as marked psychosexual upheaval take place. Despite the castration, some individuals retain the remembrance of the sex act and do not completely lose their sexual ardor. Such eunuchs have been found *in flagrante delicti*, and when so caught were strung from the battlements. The author of Ecclesiasticus knew them, for he used the simile "like a eunuch's craving to ravish a girl" (20:4). And Aristotle (384-322 B.C.), born several centuries before the apostle Matthew, knew well that "if a full-grown bull be mutilated, he can still to all appearances unite sexually with the cow."

Castration was also practiced, on farm animals and fowl, for gastronomic reasons. Caponization of the cockerel or the rooster led to fatter and more delectable fowl for eating. The changes in the personality of the rooster are striking. The normal rooster crows, struts like the king of the walk, fights other roosters for domination, chases hens, and appears to show off his comb and wattles. Following caponization, he is docile, his comb and wattles shrink, his crowing stops, he loses his aggressiveness, and he not only plays with the hens but even, poor male that he is, sets on their eggs.

Such observations probably led to the first scientific experiments in endocrinology. Berthold of Göttingen (1803-1861), the father of experimental endocrinology, demonstrated in 1849 that the virilizing effect of the testes was actually due to endocrine activity. He found that if the removed testes were reimplanted in a different part of their bodies, the castrated cocks retained their normal appearance, sexual vigor, aggressiveness and fighting instincts, comb and wattles. He thus proved that the testis, even though severed from its nerve supply and ducts, could still, by secreting its internal secretions into the bloodstream, influence both the organism and the personality.

The civilized world long ago abandoned the castration of human beings in order to make dependable and faithful servants. Yet in 1941 Dr. Charles Huggins reinstituted castration as an ameliorating measure in the management of advanced cancer of the prostate. Professor of Urology at the School of Medicine of the University of Chicago, he reasoned correctly that the prostate was hormone-dependent, and therefore that many prostatic cancers could be slowed in their inexorable progress by removal of the hormone support provided by the testes. In spite of the benefits to be derived from this procedure, some men hold dearer than life itself the possession of their testicles.

A form of punitive castration was revived in the concentration camps of Europe by the Nazi masters of sadism, to the everlasting shame of the Germanic peoples. Many an unfortunate inmate of Belzen and Auschwitz received x-ray irradiation of the testes during protective imprisonment. Two such men, now living in the United States, were seen in consultation because of severe symptoms of the male climacteric resulting from hormone deprivation. Their testes had been removed at spaced intervals of time in order to study the tissue changes induced by x-rays. In this manner was the shameless brutality of the Nazis disguised by the mask of pseudoscience.

Finally, Jesus spoke of eunuchs "which have made themselves eunuchs for the kingdom of heaven's sake." Castration did become a religious rite. For several centuries, the choir boys of the Sistine Chapel in Rome were castrated in order to preserve their soprano voices; on reaching adulthood, such singers became known as "castrati." Only in 1878, upon the accession of Pope Leo XIII, was the Italian practice of castrating boys in order to train them as adult soprano singers brought to an end. Such famous voices as those of Caffarelli, Velluti, and Farinelli owed their success to the abominable operation which now, fortunately, has been wholly abandoned.

In early Christian times, acting on the texts of Matthew, others voluntarily emasculated themselves, or permitted the operation to be performed on them, in order to avoid sexual temptation or sin. By the third century, a sect of eunuchs arose, the Valesii, whom Augustine describes as believing that their castration aided them to serve God. Their interpretation and practice were vehemently denounced and never officially approved by the Roman Church. Nevertheless, religious sects have cropped up from time to time for whom castration was a rite. In 1771 such a sect, known as the Skoptsi, was discovered to exist in Russia. Their leader, Selvinov, mutilated himself as an act of salvation; he died in 1832 in his hundredth year. In 1874, it is said, the Skoptsi had more than 5,000 members. Persecuted by the Russians, they fled to Rumania. Whether this order still exists, I do not know; but this much appears certain, that the phrase spoken figuratively by Jesus of Nazareth and recorded by Matthew was taken to heart by religious fanatics in various climes and times. Jesus merely called upon those who could do so to forsake the pleasures of the flesh and to follow him.

The word *eunuch* appears twenty-six times in the King James version of the Holy Bible. Because of the confidence they gained from their relationship to men of importance, to kings and to princes, eunuchs frequently attained considerable stature themselves. Luke, the physician, recorded in the Book of Acts the account of the early missionary Philip, who was divinely led to help a traveler understand the Scriptures. Luke states that the traveler was a "eunuch of great authority under Candace queen of the Ethiopians, who had the charge of all her treasure" (Acts 8:26-39). And the word eunuch, especially in Egypt, was even applied to noncastrated, but loyal, servants and administrators of the king.

Although castration was a custom in the Orient, in the Middle East, and later in Greece and in the Roman Empire, it was not practiced by the Hebrews, according to the famous historian Josephus, on either men or animals. In all probability, Jesus would not condone so inhumane a practice as castration, for He must have known well the injunction in Deuteronomy (23:1), that the castrate "shall not enter into the congregation of the Lord."

Abraham and the angels.

9

Testament, Testimonial and Testicle

And Abraham said unto his eldest servant of his house, that ruled over all that he had, Put, I pray thee, thy hand under my thigh:
And I will make thee swear by the Lord, the God of heaven, and the God of the earth, that thou shalt not take a wife unto my son of the daughters of the Canaanites.   Genesis 24:2-3

What relationship exists between taking an oath and the genitals? Why did young men of old swear on their manhood? Whence came the custom of swearing an oath on some sacred or revered object—such as the Bible?

I SWEAR BY APOLLO the physician, and Aesculapius and Hygeia and Panacea and all the gods and godesses"—thus the fledgling physician enters into a pact with mythological Greek gods that he will abide by the ethical code prescribed by the great Hippocrates for the practitioners of the healing art of medicine. To enter into convenants with the gods dates back many millenia. When the Egyptians first began to record on stone and papyrus their codes and laws, their exploits and accomplishments, their fables and foibles, such agreements were so important that they were made with gods—and thereby, of course, with people.

According to the funerary papyri, Princess Nesi-Khensu, ten centuries before Christ, contracted with the god, Amen-Ra, to grant her certain favors in the Other World in return for her zeal and devotion. A thousand years earlier, Abraham entered into a covenant with the Lord and sealed it through circumcision. Circumcision represented a holy bond between the Lord God and this man. It is of little surprise, therefore, that Abraham in demanding an oath of his servant, bid him place his hand "under his thigh," just as today we place our hand over the heart in swearing allegiance to the flag. "Under the thigh" was, of course, a euphemism.

49

Why the reverence for the genital zone? Early religion, one must recall, was based on the generative impulse. The power of reproduction was of foremost importance and gave direction and consequence to religious fancies. Fecundity, of man and beasts, and fertility of the soil, were the mainsprings of his existence, and primitive man consecrated and sanctified the organ of reproduction. He interpreted the natural phenomena about him and wove them into the imaginative social fabrics of his civilization. Day and night, the waxing and waning of the moon, the recurrent seasons, planting and harvesting, birth, death, rebirth—these fascinated him and gave meaning to his little universe. The fertility cult was grounded in the basic hopes, aspirations and prayers of his survival.

Abraham was strongly influenced by the cults, which were an integral part of the way of life of the people about him and to whose culture he had been exposed. The very mode of administering the oath that he employed was not an isolated incident, for later in Genesis we learn:

> And the time drew nigh that Isreal [Jacob] must die: and he called his son Joseph, and said unto him, If now I have found grace in thy sight, put, I pray thee, thy hand under my thigh, and deal kindly and truly with me: bury me not, I pray thee, in Egypt.   Genesis 47:29

The walls of Egyptian temples of antiquity bear witness to the importance of the phallic symbol in the mores of that period. Gods, kings and great men were depicted often with penis erectus. Later, this image was translated into the obelisk, one of their popular forms of monumental design. The obelisks were much admired by the Roman emperors, and many were carried off; today they may be viewed in Rome, Constantinople, London and New York. One of the most famous, built by Rameses II at Luxor in Egypt, *circa* 1250 B.C., was transported to Paris in 1831, and five years later was erected in the Place de la Concorde. But the biggest obelisk of them all was built as a testimonial to "the father of his country," our own George Washington. The Washington Monument measures over 555 feet in height and over 55 feet at the base. It is indeed a fitting memorial to a great man who was every inch a man.

Embedded in the cultures of various peoples in widely dispersed areas of the world is a relationship between an oath and the genitals. For centuries in the Western World, man took an oath by testifying "on his manhood," and indeed the Latin word "testes" is defined in *Webster's International Dictionary* as being a witness to manhood. To testify is derived from the Latin root testis. S. R. Driver, in the *Westminster Commentary*, suggests that the Australian aborigines swore amity and willingness to aid one another by one man's sitting on the other's thighs. It is recorded that when the chief of the Sioux Indians demanded a count of the loyal warriors in his tribe, those who dropped their loin cloths did so in affirmation of their fealty.

It would appear that the custom of making a contract, taking an oath, or entering into a convenant (the literal meaning of "testament") by reference to the groin (scrotum or testes) is an ancient and common one, at any rate not confined only to the early Jews. It is found in a great number of primitive societies. This primitive form of oathtaking was long ago abandoned by the Jews and was replaced by swearing on a sacred object, such as the scrolls of the Torah (the five books of Moses). Throughout the Anglo-Saxon world, taking an oath on the Holy Bible has become a thoroughly ingrained practice in courts of law.

In searching the scriptures, one learns that *covenant* appears many times in both Old and New Testaments (King James version), but that *testament*, used interchangeably with *covenant* in the New, does not appear at all in the Old. The first mention of *covenant* is in connection with Noah:

> But with thee will I establish my covenant; and thou shalt come into the ark, thou, and thy sons, and thy wife, and thy sons' wives with thee.
>
> Genesis 6:18

Testament first appears in Matthew's Gospel "For this is my blood of the new testament, which is shed for many for the remission of sins" (Matthew 26:28). *Testimony*, on the other hand, appears in both books, "And he gave unto Moses, when he had made an end of communing with him upon mount Sinai, two tables of testimony, tables of stone, written with the finger of God" (Exodus 31:18).

The modern endocrinologist has an abiding interest in reproductive physiology and the effect of the hormones of reproduction on the life of individuals and their impact on the race. The course of history may have been far different if Hitler could have fathered children. There is a substantial suspicion that Hitler was asexual—his relationships to the very few women in his life were said to be platonic only. His lack of testicular vigor indirectly played havoc with his personality, and as a consequence horridly affected our civilization. It has been said of Goering, Hitler's chief lieutenant, that he behaved like an adult eunuch; he was fat and caponlike, a change that came soon after World War I. Later, frustrated, dejected, vengeful, addicted to dope and to food, he could no longer sublimate his compulsion to ravage the human race. On the other hand, vigorous men like George Washington and Winston Churchill have been mankind's benefactors. Perhaps, an obelisk will be built one day as a testimonial to Churchill's courage and perseverance—thus covenanting the hopes and aspirations of embattled peoples the world over.

The importance of intact testicles was alluded to in Chapter 8, where mention was made that a eunuch could not enter the sanctuary. "He that is wounded in the stones ... shall not enter into the congregation of the Lord" (Deuteronomy 23:1). This Jewish tradition was followed by the Roman Catholic Church: the sacraments of marriage and ordination were forbidden to eunuchs, and proof of intact testes became a requisite for election to the papacy.

To follow the proscription laid down in the Old Testament, legend has it that on the day of enthroning a new pope, the cardinals charged with the election of a successor to St. Peter had to verify, *de vistu et tacto*, that the "elect" indeed had testicles. According to Richard Millant in *Les Eunuques à Travers les Ages*, this task was performed while the pope, being transported on the shoulders of the canons, was seated on a marble throne with a hole in the seat. The council of cardinals then pronounced the verdict, "Testiculos habet et bene pendentes."

There is a story, apocryphal perhaps, of a young man from the mountains of Eastern Tennessee, who still spoke an Elizabethan form of English. He applied for work in a nearby city and, when asked to present his testimonials, did so by giving evidence of his manhood. Testament, testimonial and testes, indeed, have been woven into the social fabric of our civilization.

The circumcision of Jesus as represented by Marco Marziale.

10

Token of the Covenant

This is my covenant, which ye shall keep, between me and you and thy seed after thee; Every man child among you shall be circumcised.

And ye shall circumcise the flesh of your foreskin; and it shall be a token of the covenant betwixt me and you.

And he that is eight days old shall be circumcised among you, every man child in your generations, . . .

And the uncircumcised man child whose flesh of his foreskin is not circumcised, that soul shall be cut off from his people; he hath broken my covenant.   Genesis 17:10–12, 14

Is circumcision a religious observation alone, or is it also a matter of health?

THE ORIGIN OF CIRCUMCISION is lost in time. Yet many theories have been presented concerning it: it is a blood-offering to the gods, a substitute for other sacrifice, a hygienic practice.

CIRCUMCISION

Early in the history of the Eastern civilizations, a custom in the times of crises was to offer a human sacrifice as an appeasement to the gods or to the avenging demons. The people believed that pestilence, fire, famine, flood and earthquake were evidence of deistic wrath. Human sacrifices had been generously tempered by the substitution of animals, and it was presumed that the blood of circumcision would be an acceptable form of mollification. The expiation of guilt wrought by the blood of an individual has remained a ritualistic practice among many peoples.

In torrid lands and hot climates, *balanitis, phimosis,* and various other forms of inflammation involving the *prepuce* were common; and as protection against them, a form of surgical interference evolved. Cutting off the useless appendage with a sharp stone guarded against later irritation and inflammation, consequences of habitual uncleanliness. Circumcision mitigated the occurrence of unnecessary ills and complications and was an aid to personal cleanliness. Tribal experience found it healthful, and it was transliterated into a form of religious purification.

Among the ancient Egyptians, circumcision was at first performed on the priestly class, then adopted by the warriors and the nobility. When Joseph became overlord of Egypt, he extended the benefits of this procedure, some scholars believe, to include the general populace. To attain this goal, he promised the Egyptians food during the famine if they would submit to circumcision. If he did so, he was the first bureaucrat to tie social security to measures for public health.

The Jews held circumcision to be of profound religious significance, for it represented the fulfillment of the Covenant between God and Abraham. With them, it became a deep-rooted custom that they could not be forced to relinquish, even during the conquest of Judea by the Greeks, and later by the Romans. It was ineradicable: when Antiochus tried to prevent the practice, mothers allowed themselves to be put to death rather than to give up the circumcision of their sons. Some rich, young, Hellenized Jews were embarrassed to frequent the public baths and gymnasia because of the stigma of circumcision; but others used it as a badge of courage.

Though John the Baptist and Jesus were circumcised according to the Law, a serious disagreement divided the early Christians. The Christians of Judea could not conceive of being converted to the new faith without submitting to the Law.

And certain men which came down from Judea taught the brethren, and said, Except ye be circumcised after the manner of Moses, ye cannot be saved.
Acts 15:1

All of the Apostle Paul's tenacity and persuasiveness were necessary to prevent circumcision from being made a condition to membership in the New Order. It was decided not to put a yoke upon the neck of the disciples, not to insist on circumcision—an alien concept, difficult for the Gentiles to accept. Thus the Apostles settled for the following minimum, but necessary things, so as to lay upon them no greater burden: "That ye abstain from meats offered to idols, and from blood, and from things strangled, and from fornication: from which if ye keep yourselves, ye shall do well" (Acts 15:29). As Christianity spread through the Occident, circumcision was all but lost to the Christian world. Yet in the last few decades, pediatricians and obstetricians have revived its practice throughout the western world.

CIRCUMVENTION

Many years ago, visiting St. Peter's Hospital for Stone, in London, I was spectator of a difficult surgical operation for genital malignancy. The gray-haired surgeon remarked that, in his long experience, he had never encountered penile cancer in a Jew. I pondered this observation, searched through the literature, and found the case report of a Jew who did suffer from this form of cancer; however, born and bred in a small town in Nebraska, he did not have the rite available to him and was never circumcised. On further inquiry, I learned that in India, genital cancer is much more frequent in the Hindu than in the Mohammedan; the latter is circumcised as a ritual of puberty.

Circumcision is a worthwhile procedure, it would appear, if for no other reason than its prophylactic value. But there is greater import to this observation than is immediately apparent, and that concerns the epidemiology of cancer of the mouth of the womb, that is, the cervix. Nuns and virginal women rarely have cervical cancer, thus incriminating a factor of married life, coitus.

According to a ten–city survey, the incidence of cancer of the cervix in American white women is 35.2 per 100,000, in American nonwhite women, 61.2 per 100,000. In Israeli women, the rate is 2.2 per 100,000, and this exceedingly low rate is matched by studies on Jewish women in the United States. The significance of these facts has not been appreciated fully. Among women in most Latin and South American countries and among Hindu women in India, cancer of the cervix accounts for about forty per cent of all malignancies in the female. The most likely common denominator is the introduction through coitus by the uncircumcised sexual partner of a cancer irritant or virus.

There is almost certainly more to circumcision that mere ritual. The historic experience of the peoples inhabiting the Fertile Crescent and the lands bordering the shores of the eastern Mediterranean has provided a clue that may contribute much to unraveling the *pathogenesis* and *epidemiology* of both penile and cervical cancer.

CIRCUMSPECTION

There may have been other motives for circumcision. The foreskin protects the sensitive *corona* and *glans*. Exaggerated sensibility of these structures may initiate a train of reactions, in the unconscionable and undisciplined individual, detrimental to the mores of society. Circumcision permits greater *cornification* and thus diminishes the *hyperesthesia* of the glans. By dulling the edge of sensuousness, man is better able to bridle his passions and to adjust his sexual behavior to conform to convention.

The priapic preoccupation of the early Israelites with the foreskin was inspired as much by the goal of survival as by reasons spiritual and aesthetic. Through trial and error, the forerunners of our Judeo-Christian civilization learned of the expediency of circumcision; it became a religious rite, but it was a good public health measure.

Esau selling his birthright to Jacob in return for a plate of pottage.

11

At the Point to Die

And Jacob sod [boiled] pottage: and Esau came from the field, and he was faint:

And Esau said to Jacob, Feed me, I pray thee, with that same red pottage; for I am faint . . .

And Jacob said, Sell me this day thy birthright.

And Esau said, Behold, I am at the point to die: and what profit shall this birthright do to me?

. . . and he sold his birthright unto Jacob.   Genesis 25:29-33

Did Esau sell his birthright cheaply, as the Scriptures suggest, despising it? Or did he have a physiologic need greater than that for his birthright?

MORE OFTEN MISREAD than any other Bible story, perhaps, is that of Esau, heir to his family birthright because he was born before his twin brother, Jacob. This elder son of Isaac and Rebekah is maligned as an insensitive glutton who unhesitatingly traded his most precious possession for a mere bowl of pottage. Yet none suggests that he wanted either intelligence or ambition: surely such a man would have appreciated the honors and possessions that his birthright assured to him.

Esau's words of assent to Jacob's hard bargain are dramatic for the modern endocrinologist, and for his patients. "Behold," he said, "*I am at the point to die:* and what profit shall this birthright do to me?" In almost certainty, Esau was the victim of an illness recognized only in recent times: *hypoglycemia,* or low blood sugar.

The discovery of the hormone *insulin* in 1921 by the late Sir Frederick Grant Banting, Nobel laureate, opened a great medical era. It made possible, finally, the successful management of those persons afflicted with uncontrollably high blood sugar, *diabetes mellitus.*

But after physicians had employed insulin for several years, an astute clinician, Dr. Seale Harris of Alabama, observed in some of his patients signs and symptoms like those that result from an overdosage of insulin. And with Dr. Harris' observation, a new clinical entity came into being: the syndrome of low blood sugar, known as hypoglycemia.

Its symptoms vary, but most evident are hunger and a craving for sweets, sometimes accompanied by fatigue and weakness, apprehension and confusion, blackouts and even stupor. A decline in blood sugar triggers an outpouring of *adrenalin*, which so stimulates the body's sugar stores that they are released into the bloodstream. Such is our built-in adjusting mechanism that keeps our essential blood sugar at fairly constant levels.

However, as adrenalin enters the blood, it may cause palpitations of the heart, flushing and sweating, or syncope (a fainting spell). Victims feel, surely, "at the point to die." Such a victim was Esau, who seemed to know his limitations and his needs: he knew that he must have food and water instantly, or drop. He really had little choice between trading his birthright for the mess of pottage and getting well, or going without the pottage and suffering the ignominy, for a cunning hunter, of total collapse. Observe how readily he recovered:

Then Jacob gave Esau bread and pottage of lentiles; and he did eat and drink, and rose up, and went his way: thus Esau despised his birthright.

Genesis 25:34

Did Esau indeed despise his birthright? Formerly, the diet given to one threatened by an impending attack of low blood sugar was food rich in *carbohydrates* and starches. But many years of experimenting with diets proved that the longtime management of the disorder depended not on high carbohydrates but on high *protein* feedings. The protein-rich lentil soup that Esau craved provided a clue long unnoticed and so unheeded.

Sugar-starvation is a strange illness, and until Dr. Harris defined it in 1924, it belonged in the category described by Camillo in *The Winter's Tale* (I, 2):

There is a sickness
Which puts some of us in distemper; but
I cannot name the disease. . . .

Even today its diagnosis is often missed because of the extreme variability of its manifestations. The occurrence of functional hypo-

62

glycemia, although frequent enough, is understood so poorly that the disorder has earned the sobriquet, "stepchild of medicine."

It is marked by an increased output of, or increased sensitivity to, endogenously produced insulin. This sensitivity is intensified by emotional turmoil and stress, by constant pressure and by violent exercise. We know today that the syndrome of low blood sugar stems from various endocrine disorders—pituitary gland failure, severe *hypothyroidism* (myxedema), exhaustion of the adrenal glands (Addison's disease)—but that the most severe cases are caused by the somewhat rare insulin-producing tumors of the pancreas.

Recently, hypoglycemia has been recognized as a complication in some cases of *congenital adrenal hyperplasia,* a disease that Esau might well have had. In this disease, because of an inborn error of metabolism, the adrenal gland produces an excess of hormones that virilize the female and cause the male to undergo a precocious development of secondary sexual characteristics (macrogenitosomia precox). These hormones are produced at the expense of essential cortisonelike hormones that are necessary to the body's economy in maintaining salt and water balances, and that profoundly influence the storage and utilization of sugars and of fats. Congenital adrenal hyperplasia exists in at least four types: the normal group (no apparent salt and water imbalance), the high blood-pressure group (salt-retainers, hypertensives), the salt-losers (tendency to shock and acute crises), and the low blood-sugar group (hypoglycemia).

Esau's history suggests that he was a victim of hypoglycemia, probably as a complication of congenital adrenal hyperplasia, with its associated macrogenitosomia precox. Such a child is often robust, an "infant Hercules." His early growth is rapid: his muscular development, his strength, and the size of his genitals are abnormal, his voice is extremely deep, and he is very hairy. Yet, paradoxically, in spite of all these signs of extraordinary virility, he is, like Esau, subject to sudden collapse.

The twin brothers had struggled within Rebekah's womb as they were to struggle without:

And the first came out red, all over like an hairy garment: and they called his name Esau.
And after that came his brother out . . . and his name was called Jacob . . .
And the boys grew: and Esau was a cunning hunter, a man of the field; and Jacob was a plain man, dwelling in tents.   Genesis 25:25-27

They were of startling contrast: one rough, the other polished; one a strong hunter, the other a homebody. Small wonder that "Isaac loved Esau . . . but Rebekah loved Jacob." So deep was her mother's love for her favorite son that she stooped to deceit and, that he might win the blessing of his aged and blind father, persuaded Jacob to disguise himself as his brother by dressing in goatskins.

> And Isaac said unto Jacob, Come near, I pray thee that I may feel thee, my son, whether thou by my very son Esau or not.
> And Jacob went near unto Isaac his father; and he felt him, and said, The voice is Jacob's voice, but the hands are the hands of Esau.
> And he discerned him not, because his hands were hairy, as his brother Esau's hands: so he blessed him.   Genesis 27:21-23

Having himself foresworn his birthright, Esau now lost all opportunity of recovering it.

Although low blood sugar is labeled a "modern disease," it is rooted clearly in antiquity. The body's priceless commodity, sugar fuels the cells and sustains the brain; without it, the body fails. Esau may offer us the first recorded case of hypoglycemia, and we may be impressed by his knowledge of its quick corrective—the high-protein lentil soup and bread of barley and of wheat. He was a husky huntsman, the Scripture indicates, who loved life, lived it to the hilt, and had little choice but to sell his birthright when "at the point to die."

Acts, Chap. 26, Ver. 17.

SAUL's CONVERSION.

Saul's conversion on the road to Damascus.

12

A Little Bit of Salt

And it came to pass, that, as I made my journey, and was come nigh unto Damascus about noon, suddenly there shone from heaven a great light round about me.

And I fell unto the ground. . . .   Acts 22:6-7

Did Saul of Tarsus, later Paul the Apostle, suffer from heat prostration because of depletion of salt and water, or from something else?

THE COURSE OF HISTORY has often been altered by some unforseen event, some psychophysical happenstance or ailment occuring in an individual destined to influence the lives of his own and future generations. It is said that Napoleon might have won the Battle of Waterloo had he not been so discommoded, the previous night, by the pain and discomfort of a severe case of hemorrhoids that he was late for the battle. If the Berbers in Africa had not revolted against the Arabs soon after Charles Martel stopped the invading Mohammedan hordes at Poitiers in 732 (Battle of Tours), Martel might not have contained the surging Moslems and thus saved Europe for Christendom. If Saul of Tarsus, tormentor of those Jews who had accepted Jesus of Nazareth as their Messiah, had not fainted on his journey to Damascus, he might not have undergone conversion to the New Order and become Christianity's great protagonist.

Let us examine the circumstances of Saul of Tarsus' frightening experience under the relentless noonday sun, while on his long and arduous journey to Damascus from Jerusalem.

Brooding over the manner in which he had persecuted his fellow Jews, Saul was impressed by their turn the other cheek attitude to his abuse. He probably drank little and ate little while on this journey. In all probability, he was the victim of heat prostration owing to depletion of salt and water. What was uppermost in his subconscious came to the fore as he heard a voice saying: "Saul, Saul, why persecutest thou me?" (Acts 9:4) Because of the aura—the forewarning that comes before an epileptic seizure, in this case the "great light"—students of the life of Paul have ascribed this disorder to him. Did Saul of Tarsus suffer an epileptic attack? Recovery from an attack is ʼusually a matter of minutes. But in Saul's case, the severe and damaging effect of heat prostration lasted three days. He was in a stupor and so grievously affected that during this time "he was three days without sight, and neither did eat nor drink" (Acts 9:9). Later, relating his experience to Agrippa, Paul once more emphasized that the spell occurred at midday while the sun was very bright.

At midday, O king, I saw in the way a light from heaven, above the brightness of the sun, shining round about me and them which journeyed with me.   Acts 26:13

So eloquent and convincing was Paul concerning his mission and his fealty to his heavenly vision that Agrippa is reported to have said: "Almost thou persuadest me to be a Christian" (Acts 26:28).

In all hot climates, the syndrome of heat exhaustion from salt and water depletion is common. Heat exhaustion presents a typical picture of salt depletion—muscular weakness, headache, giddiness, tendency to faint on standing, loss of appetite, nausea, vomiting, cramps, mental confusion and delusions. The treatment is salt replacement, and today salt tablets are provided for those exposed to strenuous work or exercise in the heat. Incidentally, long before adrenal cortical hormones become available, Dr. Robert Loeb managed his patients with Addison's disease by advising a marked increase in salt intake. Dr. H. L. Marriott of London, England, in his book *Salt and Water Depletion*, relates that during a tour of duty in India, 1,959 men were hospitalized because of heat prostration, and 136 died.

The body's electrolyte balance can be seriously injured in hot atmospheric conditions by loss of water and salt from sweating, overheating from cessation of sweating accompanied by a very high fever (hyperpyrexia), or water depletion without salt loss. If neither water nor food is taken, the effects of water depletion dominate the picture; unavoidable water losses continue while salt loss is relatively slight. The body economizes salt more effectively than water. Pure water depletion occurs in the shipwrecked and those lost in the desert.

The importance of salt and water balance in the body economy may be judged from the fact that the imbalance may readily terminate in death. Salt and water are so closely associated in the body that their constancy must be maintained at precise levels by a most intricate system of checks and double checks. The posterior pituitary gland's antidiuretic hormone conserves water; the adrenal cortical hormones, aldosterone and other corticoids, conserve sodium (salt); and the kidneys preserve the chemical balance in the body by monitoring the resorption or elimination of necessary elements.

We live in an "internal sea" of fluids. Our entire internal environment passes through the kidneys fifteen times a day. Approximately 1,700 quarts of blood flow through the kidneys every day, but only one-thousandth is converted to urine. Far less dramatic than the throbbing of the restless heart are the Herculean labors of the kidneys. Their task is prodigious but silent, regulating the vital salt and water balances within extremely narrow limits compatible with life. About two and one-half pounds of salt pass through the kidney tubules daily, but only a little less than one-third of an ounce is excreted in the urine. Thus our internal sea, the body fluids, serves as an ever-present reminder of our marine ancestory.

Before their first stirring in the primeval slime, the extremely remote ancestors of man lived in the briny deep. To come ashore, they had to establish an enclosed aqueous medium that would carry on the role of sea water. That man's forebears evolved from the sea may be assumed from man's developing a most complex and remarkable system in order to maintain the internal environment—in a fashion to match, more or less, the salinity of his ancient abode.

Snively points out, in his excellent *Sea Within: The Story of our Body Fluid,* that our chemical ancestry can be traced ultimately to the earth, for the chemical properties that made it possible for life to arise in the sea were washed there from the solid earth. Jesus of Nazareth meant more than it seemed when he said, in the Sermon on the Mount: "Ye are the salt of the earth" (Matthew 5:13).

We can rejoice with the Psalmist who with solemn reverence sang: "How manifold are thy works, O Lord," when we learn of the crucial role that the body fluids play in the physiologic drama of our daily lives. The very body fluid, described as converted sea water, is delicately brought into balance despite the extreme changes in atmospheric conditions and food intake.

Salt's essential usefulness to man caused it to be referred to often in the Bible, literally and figuratively. Salt has played a decided role in the history of mankind. It was greatly valued in the preservation of fish and meat and as a dietary supplement. In lands in which cereal foods are the main source of nutrition and the diet is poor in salt, the addition of salt is necessary to maintain vigorous health. The importance of the supplementary salt became part of the religious custom of the ancient Jews, and to this day the salting of the first morsel of bread as part of the grace before a meal is followed by Orthodox Jews throughout the world. The preservative qualities of salt made it a peculiarly fitting symbol of an enduring race ("a covenant of salt . . ." Numbers 18:19).

Salt held great economic importance. It was the main source of trade between many nations. In Oriental countries, salt taxes were so heavy that the article was not infrequently mixed with inert materials and reached the consumer in an impure state. The reference in Matthew "if the salt have lost his savour" (5:13) takes on meaning. In the Roman army, an allowance of salt was given to the officers and men. This "salarium" had the equivalence of money. The expression "not worth his salt" may be equated with "not worth his salary". One of the oldest roads in Italy is the Via Salaria, by which the produce of the salt pans of Ostia was carried into the Sabine country.

The word *salt* is sprinkled throughout the entire Bible. It is found in both Old and New Testaments, appearing over thirty-five times. A land sowed with salt became uninhabited and useless (Deuteronomy 29:22-23). A land abundant in salt reserves was chosen by Moses for the Children of Israel as the Promised Land.

And as for the western border, ye shall even have the great sea for a border: this shall be your west border . . .
And the border shall go down to Jordon, and the goings out of it shall be at the salt sea: this shall be your land with the coasts thereof round about.
Numbers 34:6,12

The role of salt in the health and survival of his people was of consummate importance to Moses. Moses led the Children of Israel to the land of promise; he understood well the arid country, the intense heat, the heavy labors and struggles ahead. As an Egyptian prince, he observed the fatigue, heat exhaustion and death that came to the Israelitish slaves who toiled in the broiling sun, preparing "bricks without straw" (Exodus 5:7) for their Egyptian masters. Fully aware of the necessity of salt to the health of his people, he made salting part of the rites and rituals for the preparation of food, especially meat. The availability of salt tablets to men working in great heat is now saving countless lives.

It appears that a little bit of salt or the lack of it may have changed the course of history. Saul, after collapsing in the noonday sun, was compelled by the voice he heard and the vision he saw to convert to the New Order.

It must be recalled that by the time Saul of Tarsus took on his evangelistic mission, James, the brother of Jesus, was already established as the leader of a small but active community in Jerusalem. Though the early followers believed in Jesus as the Messiah (Christos), they were observant Jews according to the law of Moses (Acts 21:20). Neither James nor Peter was wholly in accord with the aggressive policies advocated by Saul, soon to be known as Paul. His goal was to bring the message to a larger arena of people—the Gentiles. With indefatigable zeal he set out to accomplish his purpose amid unbelievable hardships and considerable hostility, by presenting the new *ethic* in a more palatable and acceptable form.

We will never know what might have been the course of history if James had had his way. Peter reluctantly accepted the Pauline doctrine. This much is certain, that the dramatic change in Saul's cerebation was indirectly responsible for the seeding and growth of Christianity throughout the Mediterranean World.

The writing on the wall at Belshazzar's feast.

13

Signs and Symbols

For nothing is secret, that shall not be made manifest; neither any thing hid, that shall not be known and come abroad.   Luke 8:17

Whence come symbols? Are they the secrets of the past speaking to us? Do we know their meanings?

SIGNS AND SYMBOLS leave their stamp on posterity. An idea portrayed by a mark, letter, work, emblem, insignia, or other token may serve as a symbol. If attached to it are some attributes and it sparks the imagination and arouses the emotions, anything may be symbolic. Symbolism may involve the art of selecting, consciously or unconsciously, analogies for the abstract. Most familiar to us are flags and coats of arms, school and college crests, and symbols connected with certain ideologies and religions. Although symbols are a great part of our world, we seldom realize their impact on our thoughts and our actions.

Symbols are the common language of people, literate and illiterate, the world over. They are a language that incites and excites, implies and implores, informs and stirs, often plumbing deep wells of emotion. Their original meanings often lie lost beneath the dusts of centuries. For example, at one time a red shield marked both the home and place of business of a petty banker—Mayer Amschel of Frankfurt-on-Main. In translation, the house with the red shield is now the "House of Rothschild." In Germanic countries, a green leaf ("grune blatt") was the hallmark of a hostelry or inn, where it was possible to learn the events taking place in both neighboring communities and the outside world. Thus, it follows logically that a widely read German weekly— a scandal or gossip sheet carried on in the tradition of a news-gathering hostelry of old—is known as the *Grune Blatt*. The sign of the three golden balls, which today is displayed outside the pawnbroker's shop, was the proud "neon sign" of the first bankers of the modern world, the Medici family of Florence.

What does Rx on a prescription mean to the average physician, medical student, or pharmacist? Whence the insignia of the general's star, the colonel's eagle, or the major's cluster of oak leaves? How did the caduceus—the rod entwined by one or two snakes—become the emblem of the healing arts?

Among the best-known symbols today is the physician's emblem— "Rx"—which has been employed since ancient times. It is believed that this was originally the symbol of *Marduk,* god of wisdom, who became Babylon's chief divinity. His sign was placed on prescriptions by Babylonian physicians, who used it as an invocation to him. Such a practice can be traced back to more than ten centuries before the Christian Era. It is probable that a general's star was adopted, perhaps unconsciously, from an ancient belief that stars held a special power. In fact, stars were worshipped by the people of certain nations, including Egypt and Chaldea. The Chaldeans, interested in astrology, revered the stars, and their brilliance so impressed the Israelites that they made them symbols of exalted persons, such as King David, the Patriarchs, princes, rulers and nobles. Besides denoting nobility, they served as guides, as Matthew's account in his Gospel that a star in the East guided the Wise Men to the place of Jesus' birth (Matthew 2:2). Since a general is a distinguished person and a guider of men, this symbol is fitting. A full colonel's emblem, *the silver eagle,* had ever denoted greatness and power; the rapidity of an army's movements is compared with an eagle's flight in the Old Testament. Gaius Marius, a Roman general who lived during the century before the birth of Jesus, chose an eagle as the sign to be used on the banner of his legion. Under the French Empire, it became France's emblem also. The oak leaves, worn by both a lieutenant colonel and a major, can be traced far back. The tree is Israel's symbol signifying strong, powerful men. Or perhaps it was chosen because of its later connection with the famous British Oak in Sherwood Forest, called the *Major Oak* during the time of King John, son of Henry II.

Greek medicine set the stage for later centuries. The ancient Greek physicians were the priests of Aesculapius, who practiced in temples. Although Aesculapius was deified, he had been an actual man dedicated to healing, and his symbol was the *caduceus:* two snakes twined around a rod (this famed physician's name is also spelled Asklepios).

He lived during the Thirteenth Century B.C., and is honored by being included in the oath of Hippocrates taken by medical students. The physician's insignia, the caduceus, might have originated from the belief held by ancient Greeks that serpents were divine and associated with the art of healing. Therefore, snakes were housed in the temple of Asklepios. That great physician is depicted as holding a rod, around which a snake is curled. Greek mythology contains numerous stories of serpents with healing powers. The rod was supposedly given to Mercury, herald of the gods; poets have written that it brought sleep. In *Paradise Lost*, John Milton termed it "his opiate rod." During the eighteenth century, Erasmus Darwin wrote of Hermes (the Greek predecessor of the Roman Mercury) as using his "dread caduceus" as a means of rescue "From the dark regions of the imprisoned dead. . . ." Possibly the roots from which the symbol of the caduceus originally sprang mingled magic with religion. Today, it bears a different significance: the snakes indicate "wisdom in healing," and the rod or staff is a token of "comfort and compassion." This emblem was employed by the Royal Army Medical Corps and later became the emblem of The United States Army Medical Corps. Thus, antiquity reaches toward our day through the common language of symbolism.

Subconsciously, words, paintings, designs and architectural structures are part of the language of symbolism. The cross in early civilizations signified solar light. The vestments of the priests of Horus, the Egyptian god of light, were marked with a cross. It was the monogram, too, of Osiris, the chief Egyptian god, and implied Nature's productive force. With the crucifixion of Jesus, the cross became the symbol of Christianity. The swastika, a design revered in ancient India, was once a token of health and happiness, but the cross twisted into the shape of a swastika, adopted by Nazi Germany, will be remembered for a thousand years as a symbol of hate, of the abrogation of human rights and of contempt for the dignity of man.

One's consciousness seems to be a ceaseless flow of symbols, and unconscious energies continuously seek expression. From man's earliest times on earth, he has sought in one way or another to portray his idea of God and of sex. Is the lofty church spire transmuted phallic worship? Is the dome of the mosque the subsconscious expression of a woman's nurturing breasts? Is the inverted triangle, the emblem of the YMCA, an imitation or replica of the female escutcheon? After all, the early Jewish Christians veered from a rugged and militant

75

philosophy to a credo that emphasized such attributes as love, kindness, compassion, faith, hope, charity, turning the other cheek and peace above all things.

These virtues were urged on the Gentiles, who frequently were unprepared to receive them. Some nineteen centuries later, the female escutcheon—pure and inviolate, representing femininity and gentility—was unconsciously translated into a symbol of communal welfare and endeavor. And what of the significance of the star of David, emblematic of many Jewish organizations today? Was the six-pointed star subconsciously allied with the male escutcheon in its equation with virility and fertility? Perhaps the male escutcheon superimposed on the female remains an historic reminder of the fertility cults that flourished in ancient times and was the font of man's earliest religious experiences.

Indeed, symbols speak to us from out of the past with nuances that words cannot intone.

And thou shalt bind them for a sign upon thine hand, and they shall be as frontlets between thine eyes.
And thou shalt write them upon the posts of thy house, and on thy gates.
Deuteronomy 6:8-9

This exhortation in Deuteronomy was taken literally. An amulet containing passages from the Scriptures is to this day worn on the forehead and arm of many Orthodox Jews during their morning prayers. It is a symbol of a covenant with the Lord to keep his commandments for a better life and a better world.

We are in continuous need of reminders—how else can we explain the phenomenon of the Beatles other than as a symptom of our times? We live, we say, in a sick, sick, sick world; but is it sicker than other times? Has there ever been an era when the forces of good were not challenged by the forces of evil? Conflict—national and inter-national—follows closely upon conflict; one hate group emerges as another agonizingly dies, and world crises on end bring us to the brinks of many wars. Hate often seems stronger than love, and justice unceasingly tries to catch up with injustice. Yet man's compassion for his fellow man can surpass man's inhumanity to man. And the need for such a reminder by a fitting symbol on our gateposts has not lessened with the ages.

Many Jewish homes throughout the world have a Mezuzah—a small metal casing enclosing a passage of Scripture—as a sign on the doorpost. It serves as a welcome to "the stranger within our gates." This gesture has been perpetuated also, by some Christian orders. A small wooden symbol, a "House Blessing Cross," may be found at the rear entrance door of St. Joseph's Hospital in Augusta, Georgia–an institution administered by the Sisters of St. Joseph (Carondelet):

LORD

AND

MASTER

PROTECT THIS HOUSE

AND EVERYONE WHO GOES

IN

AND

OUT

The seven-branched candlestick, Vespasian's booty from sacking the Temple in Jerusalem; AD 70. (From the Arch of Titus, Rome).

14

Seven and Seven

And at that time, Solomon held a feast, and all Israel with him, a great congregation . . . before the Lord our God, *seven* days and *seven* days, even *fourteen* days.   1 Kings 8:65

What meaning do seven *and* fourteen, *which recur throughout the Bible, shadow forth?*

FOURTEEN AND SEVEN appear often in the Old and the New Testaments, especially in the apocalyptic writings. Veiled in mystery, their uses often defy interpretation, yet both carried special meaning, clearly, in the remote past. Can it be that manifested in them as symbol is some centuries-old inheritance, from the bedrock of human experience? May the symbol be an unconscious reminder of some gratifying discovery, now all but forgotten, a haunting remnant of a joyous association of time and event? And may the endocrine system offer a key to unlock some part of our answer?

The Bible has a rich supply of these numbers; they fall into three categories: mystic, pragmatic, physiologic. Several of the New Testament uses are inscrutable. In giving the genealogy of Jesus, for example, Matthew's fourteen is considered by scholars to be symbol rather than measure of time:

So all the generations from Abraham to David are fourteen generations; and from David until the carrying away into Babylon are fourteen generations; and from the carrying away into Babylon unto Christ are fourteen generations.   Matthew 1:17

We must also read as symbol Paul's years: "I knew a man in Christ above fourteen years ago" (2 Corinthians 12:2).

Symbolic must remain the sevens of The Revelation of St. John the Divine, which is centered on seven. Its scenes are in a sevenfold structure: seven vials, plagues, trumpets, thunders, heads which are mountains; seven kings, crowns, and a slain lamb with seven horns and seven eyes. One of its clearest verses is:

The mystery of the seven stars which thou sawest in my right hand, and the seven golden candlesticks. The seven stars are the angels of the seven churches: and the seven candlesticks which thou sawest are the seven churches.
Revelation 1:20

Yet the numbers often are employed clearly and definitely. In his Epistle to the Galatians, Paul wrote: "Then fourteen years after I went up again to Jerusalem" (2:1); again in the Acts when, shipwrecked and hungry, he appeals to the passengers to partake of food: "This day is the fourteenth day that ye have tarried and continued fasting, having taken nothing" (27:33). And in the Old Testament fourteen appears with explicit meaning: the ledge of the altar shall be "fourteen cubits long and fourteen broad" (Ezekiel 43:17); Jacob served Laban fourteen years, seven for Leah, seven for Rachel (Genesis 31:41)—these from many examples.

The *Holy Days* of Judaism, which originated in Biblical times and are still celebrated, are built on sevens. The seven days of *Passover* begin at sundown on the fourteenth day of the prescribed month. The second great annual festival, the *Feast of Weeks*, begins seven weeks after Passover. And the third, the *Feast of Tabernacles*, is held in the seventh month. Most important of all is the *Sabbath*, Judaism's great contribution to human welfare, a day for rest, contemplation and worship: "And God blessed the seventh day, and sanctified it" (Genesis 2:3).

What physiologic meanings may seven and fourteen possess? Moses, the great Lawgiver, may well have understood the significance of the fourteenth day of the menstrual cycle as having something to do with fertility. He so desired the Children of Israel to multiply that he may well have contrived to increase the fertility index of Israelitish women by his ordinances of the Law of the "clean" and the "unclean":

And if a woman have an issue of her blood . . . she shall be unclean.
But if she be cleansed of her issue, then she shall number to herself seven days, and after that she shall be clean.
This is the law . . . of her that is sick of her flowers.
Leviticus 15:25,28,32–33

Women were asked to offer a sacrifice on the eighth day and encouraged to bathe in running water and be purified. Thus, after five or six days of menstruation and a waiting period of eight days, the woman was cleansed and prepared for her marital obligations, just when the likelihood of conception was greatest, on the fourteenth day of the cycle. Whether this practice was born of knowledge, prophetic vision, or of tribal experience, Moses apparently was aware of the importance of the fourteenth day of the cycle in reproduction and in the preservation of the race.

When the scribe used "seven days and seven days, even fourteen days" to describe Solomon's feast, his usage was probably less poetic modality than emphasis of an obscure symbol. Seven occurs more often than three, fourteen, or forty, the numbers heaviest with symbolism; and it seems to carry more meaning, for seven is intimately associated with the natural rhythms of nature. At four multiples of seven, the moon waxes and wanes. The periodicity of the menstrual cycle follows the lunar month. There is rhythm in the rounds of the sun, the stars and the moon, and a periodicity to many a biological phenomenon, particularly in the endocrine system. The rhythm of all human life, according to Dr. Hobart A. Reimann, may be controlled by the solar cycle of six and six-tenth days.

All these relations are pertinent to the folklore and significance of the number seven. Seven possesses magic: *seven days of creation, seven ages of man, seven deadly sins, seven joys of Mary, seventh son of seventh son, seven wonders of the world, seven seas, seventh heaven, seventh year: sabbatical, seven hills of Rome*—and seven and seven are fourteen.

Past is prologue, an introduction with a theme that is partly clear, partly blurred, partly forgotten. Its symbols, though they may seem worthless to a scientific era, speak, still. All that ever was still is. And we would do well, pausing, to turn from the demands of our days to listen and learn from that which is as old as time yet everlastingly new. So with seven and fourteen: mystical numbers, symbols, through which antiquity whispers of a buried treasury of wisdom awaiting our discernment.

Turning water into wine at the marriage feast in Cana

15

A Little Wine

Drink no longer water, but use a little wine for thy stomach's sake and
thine often infirmities.   1 Timothy 5:23

*Has man's use of wine and spirits been for his weal
or for his woe?*

WINE'S ANCIENT WORTH and its curse are mentioned almost
two hundred times in the Bible. Although the Apostle Paul's
advice to Timothy was to use wine for a medicinal purpose, its
intoxicating character was known. The "Dry Bible" substituted the
word *juice* for *wine* in order to obviate the Scriptures' slightest
encouragement to drinkers of wine.

The important role of wine in the Jewish mores and social customs is
illustrated by Jesus' first miracle. When the supply of wine ran out at
the marriage feast in Cana of Galilee, Jesus, at the behest of his
mother, turned water into "good wine," so that the festivities could
proceed (John 2:1-10). So doing, He was abiding by a Jewish custom
that holds wine to symbolize the joy and fellowship of a happy
occasion, and that, even now, is a part of the Jewish marriage
ceremony.

Because the origin of winemaking is lost in the past, we do not
know when man discovered that the juice of the grape, if allowed to
ferment, becomes wine. But we know that neolithic man, turning
from hunting to agriculture, used his crops for fermentation, and that
people in various parts of the earth learned that grapes or wet grain,
allowed to stand in warmth, became a liquor that possessed weird and
pleasant effects. Rock carvings and sketches from as early as the fourth
millenium B.C. depict the techniques used in winemaking. The world's
first biochemists, probably, were those not-so-primitive people who
concerned themselves with the fermentation of grain for beer, or of
grapes for wine.

To some early men, the blood of the grape had supernatural powers and contained, or was, a "spirit." Wine and religion were soon entwined, and wine became a part of various ritual ceremonies. At the Last Supper, when Jesus and his disciples were celebrating the Feast of the Passover, Matthew related

And he took the cup, and gave thanks, and gave it to them, saying, Drink ye all of it;
For this is my blood of the new testament, which is shed for many for the remission of sins.   Matthew 26:27-28

Thus began the practice of Holy Communion, or the Holy Eucharist, or the Lord's Supper in Christian churches.

The ancient Hebrews mixed wine and water for their beverage—"she hath mingled her wine"—and the Greeks and their cultural heirs in Rome embraced this gentle custom. In olden times, pollution of streams and wells caused frequent epidemics of cholera and of dysentery; slowly, experience passed from one generation to another that to drink water plain was hazardous. The addition of wine to water was a safety measure; to ingest mingled wine was healthful.

The reasons for the initial popularity of wines among the peoples that border the eastern and the northern shores of the Mediterranean have become dim, but the custom continues. With Gallic delight, the French have always maintained that wine is for drinking and water is for washing. A cartoon depicting a child's posterior being washed carries the legend, "La seule utilité de l'eau." Pasteur rightly described wine as the most hygienic of beverages.

The prophylactic measure of adding wine to water was thought to be a sort of myth, a popular practice handed down from antiquity. But in his charming and scientific book, *A History of Wine As Therapy,** Dr. Salvatore P. Lucia shows that it is a good deal more. Dr. Alois Pick, of the Vienna Institute of Hygiene, exposed to various mixtures of wine and water the bacilli that caused cholera and typhoid fever—two diseases transmitted by drinking water—and discovered that in them the bacilli were soon destroyed. Further, in World War II, enteric diseases spread by contaminated water presented a severe medical problem in the Mediterranean theater. An American soldier, John Gardner, was impressed by the fact that the natives, who added wine

---

*J. B. Lippincott Co., 1963.

to their water, were free from enteric diseases. Later, in a series of studies at the University of California, he found that red wines possess antibacterial properties that cannot be ascribed to their content of alcohol, aldehydes, tannins, and acids. Finally, investigations by John J. Powers at the University of Georgia, 1959, proved that other elements extracted from wines also inhibit the growth of bacteria.

That wine has antibacterial power independent of its alcohol is now well-established, and the wisdom of the ancient custom of mixing wine with water is substantiated by scientific inquiry.

Wines were drunk with meals, during festivities, and for ritual purposes, generally in moderation. But scandalous excesses did occur. The earliest reference to wine in the Bible points out that such excesses lead to confusion and abnormal behavior:

And Noah began to be a husbandman, and he planted a vineyard:
And he drank of the wine, and was drunken; and he was uncovered within his tent.   Genesis 9:20-21

Noah's sons were so embarrassed that they "covered their father's nakedness."

For health's sake and to avoid inebriation, the Hebrews had learned to dilute their wine with two parts of water; unwatered wine they considered too strong, and they permitted no blessing until the water was added. Proverbs, a poetic discourse in which man stands torn between wisdom and folly, has this to say about mingled wine:

Wisdom hath builded her house . . .
. . . she hath mingled her wine; she hath also furnished her table. . . .
As for him that wanteth understanding, she saith to him,
Come, eat of my bread, and drink of the wine which I have mingled.
Forsake the foolish, and live; and go in the way of understanding.
                                    Proverbs 9:1-2, 4-6

Wisdom dictates moderation if man would forsake the foolish. To be alive is not always to live, as physicians realize in the course of any day. Living requires concerns far more vital than biological processes only, and any excess thwarts the adventure, challenge and love that make man more than an animal. And the best can be twisted into evil; wrong usage and intemperance always haunt man.

That wine may be a tool for vice, Lot's daughters illustrate. Following the destruction of Sodom and Gomorrah, Lot and his two daughters lived in an isolated cave in the mountains. Fearful of the future, the daughters schemed:

> And the firstborn said unto the younger, Our father is old, and there is not a man in the earth to come in unto us after the manner of all the earth:
> Come, let us make our father drink wine, and we will lie with him, that we may preserve seed of our father.
> And they made their father drink wine that night: and the firstborn went in, and lay with her father; and he perceived not when she lay down, nor when she arose. Genesis 19:31-36

So, also, with the younger daughter, and thus "were both the daughters of Lot with child by their father."

The prophets took a dim view of drinking wine. One of the sternest, Hosea, spoke at a time when Israel neglected God, and his indictment is stinging:

> . . . the Lord hath a controversy with the inhabitants of the land, because there is no truth, nor mercy, nor knowledge of God in the land.
> Whoredom and wine and new wine take away the heart. Hosea 4:1, 11

The Bible denounces the immoderate use of wine. Advocating moderation in all things, Paul wrote:

> All things indeed are pure; but it is evil for that man who eateth with offence.
> It is good neither to eat flesh, nor to drink wine, nor anything whereby thy brother stumbleth, or is offended, or is made weak. Romans 14:20-21

Paul here indicates that wine is evil only if man makes it so, and that those who drink normally are not to tempt the weak. His was probably the first preventive measure suggested to curb problem drinking; his appeal is to the strong "to bear the infirmities of the weak, and not to please ourselves" (Romans 15:1).

If Paul attempted to cope with problem drinkers, Isaiah defined the source of the problem as a guide to those on the brink of or far gone in alcoholism:

> Woe unto them that rise up early in the morning, that they may follow strong drink; that continue until night, till wine inflame them!
> Woe unto them that are mighty to drink wine. . . . Isaiah 5:11, 22

We know today that the morning drinker has entered the labyrinth called alcoholism; Isaiah's picture of the night-and-day drinker is precise. But perhaps the most completely descriptive of the denunciations is that of Proverbs:

Wine is a mocker, strong drink is raging: and whosoever is deceived thereby is not wise.   Proverbs 20:1

Be not among winebibbers; among riotous eaters of flesh:
For the drunkard and the glutton shall come to poverty: and drowsiness shall clothe a man with rags.
Who hath woe? who hath sorrow? who hath contentions? who hath babbling? who hath wounds without cause? who hath redness of eyes?
They that tarry long at the wine; they that go to seek mixed wine.
Look not upon the wine when it is red, when it giveth his color in the cup, when it moveth itself aright.
At the last it biteth like a serpent, and stingeth like an adder.
                                                          Proverbs 23:20-21, 29-32

This passage is an accurate description of one who has fallen into the fearful abyss of alcoholism. It no way concerns the normal drinker, to whom alcohol is a means and not an end. Herein is the test by which one may determine whether he is a potential or even an actual alcoholic. If alcoholic beverages are but a means to one's moderate relaxation, refreshment, and stimulation, and an adjunct to hospitality, then he is hardly in danger. But if alcoholic beverages become an end, if they are a salve for one's problems, and if he drinks compulsively, then he is on treacherous land. One drink is too many—a hundred not enough.

Although general opinion has it that one becomes an alcoholic only after years of overindulgence, I believe that some persons are born with a predisposition for alcoholism, that a tendency to it is within their genetic structure. For them, warning signals flash early: they drink more than their companions, more often, more compulsively, for the wrong reasons.

Although the drinking of wine received its share of condemnation, in praise of wine the psalmist sang: "Wine that maketh glad the heart of man" (Psalm 104:15). And in Proverbs 31:4-7, King Lemuel's mother makes a nice distinction for its use:

It is not for kings, O Lemuel, it is not for kings to drink wine; nor for princes strong drink:

Lest they drink, and forget the law, and pervert the judgment of any of the afflicted.

Give strong drink unto him that is ready to perish, and wine unto those that be of heavy hearts.

Let him drink, and forget his poverty, and remember his misery no more.

Proverbs 31:4-7

The Talmud, written between 536 B.C. and A.D. 427, offers another sort of description, of a woman consuming too much wine:

One glass of wine makes the woman pretty; two glasses and she becomes hateful; at the third glass she lusts invitingly; at the fifth glass she becomes so excited that she will solicit an ass upon the streets.

This remarkable estimate one may compare with Emil Bogen's alcohol-behavior relationship: One-tenth per cent and the lady is delightful and desirable, two-tenths and she is daring and disheveled, four-tenths and she is delirious and disgusting, five-tenths and the lady is drunk. And one recalls the porter's conclusion in Macbeth (II, 3): "and drink, sir, is a great provoker, . . . it provokes the desire, but it takes away the performance."

Some centuries after Mohammed, a stirring in science and philosophy occurred in the Moslem world. The Arabs welded Judeo-Christian thought to that of the Greco-Roman civilization, and the result was an energetic inquiry into metaphysics and science. The learned sought, among more important things, to discriminate the essence of wine and to capture its hidden magic. Seeking to isolate the "spirit" of fermented juices, inquisitive Arabs of the eighth century developed a technique in which wine was heated, then cooled and condensed to prevent the vapor from escaping. The result was distilled spirits, more potent than the wine—quite unneutral "neutral" spirits.

Since the discoveries of fortifying wine and distilling liquor, the problem drinker—a problem then as now—has become more prevalent. Why is it that one person becomes drunk with one or two drinks whereas another maintains his poise even after four or five? Why is it that alcoholism is a metabolic disorder in one and a psychiatric problem for another? Our answers are not too complete.

We do know that the hypothyroid person oxidizes alcohol more slowly and is therefore more likely to become inebriated on a few drinks. The hypoglycemic person (and the hypothyroid has a distinct tendency to hypoglycemia) may inadvertently learn that alcohol, just as food or sweets, gives him a quick boost. In individuals with emotional instability, this boost may even lead to alcoholic addiction; they become psychologically conditioned to the use of alcohol as an escape mechanism. Because of malnutrition, the chronic alcoholic develops poor liver function, which interferes with the storage and release of glycogen, which leads to low blood sugar—and the vicious circle rolls on.

A relationship has been suggested between endocrine disturbances and alcoholism. In one series of problem drinkers studied, two-thirds had some degree of hypothyroidism; after thyroid therapy, their drinking patterns became less pathologic. The effect of the thyroid hormone was recently reexamined, using this time the quick-acting thyroid substance l-triiodothyronine (Cytomel). The drinkers given the hormone were clinically sober within two hours, their rate of blood-alcohol decline approximating clinical sobriety; the drinkers not given the hormone took from four to six hours to become equally sober.

Wine is cheering, nourishing and stimulating, and is probably the drug and the medicine with which humanity has had its longest experience. Wine and alcohol in moderation are a tonic to the aged, a help in promoting appetite, and a comfort to living at a time of increasing physical infirmities and diminishing satisfactions. They help to relax chronic anxieties because they placate the troubled spirit and rest the racing mind. Certainly, before science devised a variety of specifics to ameliorate diverse ailments, wine was an indispensable boon to mankind. Even in Ancient Egypt, wine was employed as a vehicle for so-called remedial agents, and many a popular nostrum today owes its success to the beneficial action of the wine or the sedative effects of the alcohol. Hippocrates recommended wine as a remedy:

Anxiety, yawning, rigor—wine drunk with an equal proportion of water, removes these complaints.

Wine is a highly complex product. Of it, Dr. Lucia writes:

As food, wine supplies fluids, calories, minerals, vitamins, proteins, and other dietary elements. As medicine, wine may act as an appetite stimulant, a stomachic, tonic, tranquilizer, anesthetic, astringent, antiseptic, vasodilator, diaphoretic, diuretic, and antibiotic agent, in addition to its age-old use as a universal menstruum for active therapeutic agents derived from plants.

And Dr. William Dock has concluded that physicians are not fully using wine at its clinical value:

> Alcohol is a good diuretic, a stimulant of gastric secretion, a dilator of blood vessels, and above all, it has an action on the mind which, by variation of dose and rate of ingestion, can bring either cheerful bustle or profound anesthesia.

Dr. Samuel Johnson knew wine, whisky, and brandy: "In the bottle," he wrote, "discontent seeks for comfort, cowardice for courage, and bashfulness for confidence." He considered that "there is no doubt that not to drink wine is a great deduction from life," and that "Wine makes a man better pleased with himself. . . . To make a man better pleased with himself, let me tell you, is doing a very great thing." But he gave it up, "till I grow old and want it," for the best of reasons: "because it is so much better for a man to be sure that he is never to be intoxicated, never to lose the power over himself."

Paul's "use a little wine for thy stomach's sake and thine often infirmities" embodies the best thought of his time. The observant Jew still offers a grace before partaking of a glass of wine: "Praised be thou, O Lord, King of the Universe, who hast created the fruit of the vine." Wine is indeed a gift from the gods, participating as it does in the sublimest of religious mysteries, though perversely contributing to the depths of human debauchery and degradation. Wine and alcohol are not the undoing of man; they are, when he permits them, his helpmeets, his servants. But they have the power to uncover the frailty of the human fabric whenever it is unable to weather the stresses and the storms of life.

The devil tempting Jesus in the desert to turn stones into bread.

16

Give Yourself to Fasting

In those days I Daniel was mourning three full weeks.
I ate no pleasant bread, neither came flesh nor wine in my mouth, neither
did I anoint myself at all, till three whole weeks were fulfilled.

Daniel 10:2-3

*Why has fasting persisted through the ages? Are its
effects harmful or beneficial?*

THE PRACTICE OF FASTING has persisted from time immemo-
rial, and it is likely to continue so long as men are capable of
religious and moral aspiration. Rooted in some of the strongest
emotions incident to human nature, it is a form of masochism
surrounded by an aura of self-denial, -purification and -sacrifice. The
first mention of fasting in the Bible concerns Moses on Mount Sinai:
for him, it was a rite of purification, of preparation for spiritual
communion.

And he was there with the Lord forty days and forty nights; he did neither
eat bread nor drink water. And he wrote upon the tables the words of the
covenant, the ten commandments.   Exodus 34:28

To endure so prolonged a fast is difficult to imagine. The fast that
Jesus undertook, when "led up of the spirit into the wilderness to be
tempted of the devil," also lasted forty days and forty nights. The
tempter asked Jesus to command stones to be made bread. His answer
reverberated down the ages: "Man shall not live by bread alone"
(Matthew 4:4). In early times, the ascetic, in his efforts to subdue
carnal desires, withdrew from all distractions of daily life and
abstained, wholly or in part, from food; he hoped thereby to be free
for spiritual thought and introspection. Fasting was a part of the
religious ritual of many of the ancient cultures; the Old and the New

Testaments mention it approximately seventy-four times. Penitential fasting is found today particularly in the Jewish and Christian faiths.

In Islam, the fast of Ramadan is a universally observed thirty-day sunup to sundown self-imposed period of food restriction, a modified fast. Buddhists find fasting appropriate to their way of contemplation and asceticism.

In different lands and ages, the practice of fasting has been differently applied. The New Testament records ". . . for there lie in wait for him of them more than forty men, which have bound themselves with an oath, that they will neither eat nor drink till they have killed him . . ." (Acts 23:21). Among the Celts, it was not uncommon for a man who was refused a lawful request to "fast against" the one who had denied him his right.

In more recent times, fasting has been used as a means of protest against alleged injustice, legal or political—namely, the hunger strike. A notable example was that of Viterbi, the Corsican lawyer condemned to death for political causes. Viterbi went on a hunger strike and provided, through a carefully kept diary, an inkling of the effects of voluntary privation. On the third day of fasting, he noted that the sensation of hunger departed, and although thereafter thirst came and went, his hunger never returned. His death occurred on the eighteenth day.

The most renowned faster of modern times was Mahatma Gandhi. In his passive resistance to the British rule of India, he engaged in fifteen fasts, three of them lasting for twenty-one days. He usually had for sustenance only hot water, sometimes with lime juice, and although he grew very weak, he remained mentally alert and suffered no lasting ill effects. Terence MacSwiney, the Irish patriot and Lord Mayor of Cork, protested his sentence of two years' imprisonment by the British by going on a diet of water alone for sixty-nine days. He died a martyr's death in October, 1920, but not because of his fasting: he died of pulmonary tuberculosis aggravated by his long deprivation of nourishment. Fasting is for the obese relatively easy; for the lean it is far more difficult.

Observations were made on the prolonged fasts of "professional fasters" toward the end of the last century. Scientific studies of the physiology of hunger and of the metabolic and psychologic changes that occur on prolonged fasting were started both in this country and abroad early in this century. In 1915, Benedict published the results of

94

his studies of a man who, drinking only distilled water, fasted for thirty-one days. About the same time, Cannon, professor of physiology at Harvard, was carrying on his monumental studies on the effects of fear, rage, pain and hunger on the body economy. Cannon showed the concept "hunger increases as time passes" to be erroneous:

On the contrary, there is abundant evidence that the sensation is not thus intensified. During continued fasting, hunger, at least in some persons, wholly disappears after the first few days.

Four or five decades passed before the fruits of such studies were clinically applied. Dr. Walter Bloom demonstrated that total fasting with free access to water was tolerated well and, in fact, most beneficial as an introduction to the treatment of obesity. More recently, Dr. Garfield Duncan and his associates corroborated Bloom's work and gave evidence of the practicable application of intermittent periods of total fasting, except for non-nutritious fluids. Such fasting was followed within a few days by *anorexia* and frequently by *euphoria*. Low caloric diets failed because they stimulated hunger rather than anorexia. Furthermore, the loss of salt and of water noted on total fasting failed to occur on low caloric diets. The impression that hunger stressed the individual, resulting in increased corticoid activity by the adrenals, thus heightening catabolism or breakdown of tissue proteins, was not substantiated by hormone assays performed before and after total fasting periods of four to fourteen days. A relationship was found, however, between the anorexia and the degree of ketosis (a mild form of acidosis in the faster's bloodstream).

Modern medical science, examining this ancient practice of total fasting, has found that it is a safe, painless, effective method for the obese individual, if undertaken for one to several weeks while under the care of a physician. It helps him to mobilize fat, which burns or is metabolized into fatty acids—hence the ketosis. Only the preoccupation of man with eating at regular intervals has led to the misconception that fasting is unpleasant. However, it is most difficult for the lean to fast, since they have little fat reserve; it must have been a particularly difficult trial for men such as Gandhi and MacSwiney. In the lean, the ketones, which lessen hunger, are not produced as they are in the obese, in whom fats are readily mobilized.

Obesity is a menace to health and happiness. Nevertheless, Shakespear, in alluding to the fat and the lean in *Julius Caesar* (I, 2), lets Caesar

95

epitomize an opinion held by scholar and layman alike ever since man started to record his ideas in picture and word. The consensus of myth, legend, history and drama has overwhelmingly equated obesity with good-naturedness and leanness with shrewd, self-critical, calculating ruthlessness.

> Let me have men about me that are fat;
> Sleek-headed men and such as sleep o'nights.
> Yond Cassius has a lean and hungry look;
> He thinks too much: such men are dangerous.

Voluntary fasting, an age-old practice, has become a therapeutic tool in the control of intractable obesity. Fasting for ten to fourteen days, given access to water, is neither archaic nor barbaric. It is tolerated well by obese men and women, and is a revolutionary and promising approach to the management of obesity.

Hermaphrodite.

98

17

Fallen Angel

When I consider thy heavens, the work of thy fingers, the moon and the stars, which thou hast ordained;

What is man, that thou art mindful of him? and the son of man, that thou visitest him?

For thou hast made him a little lower than the angels, and hast crowned him with glory and honour.   Psalm 8:3-5

What is man; what is woman; and what are the physiologic errors each is heir to?

THE IMPORTANCE of "What is man, that thou art mindful of him?" may be judged from the fact that it is one of the few passages to be found, word for word, in both the Old and the New Testaments (Hebrews 2:6-7). The two aspects of man ever have been the concern of the civilized world: man's soul and man's body. Out of the mouths of babes come queries that tax the ingenuity of scholars, such as that of the little child: "What is an angel?" I am sure that the query is directed at the physical appearance and the gender of an angel, not at his ethereal and spiritual qualities.

But when the philosopher poses the question, "What is man?", I know of no better reply than that of Homer Smith: "As a fallen angel, man would be ludicrous. As an intelligent animal he has reason to be proud, because he is the first who can ask himself, Whither, Why, and Whence?"

The poet, the historian, the social anthropologist do not inquire of physical man only, but of man endowed with a soul. God breathed life into the nostrils of man and placed him in a position a little lower than the angels, exhorting him to seek truth, do justly, love mercy, and walk humbly with his God. These things men should be and do, as Tennyson's King Arthur instructs the last of his knights, Sir Bedivere:

If thou shouldst never see my face again,
Pray for my soul. More things are wrought by prayer
Than this world dreams of. Wherefore, let thy voice
Rise like a fountain for me night and day.
For what are men better than sheep or goats
That nourish a blind life within the brain,
If, knowing God, they lift not hands of prayer
Both for themselves and those who call them friend.
for so the whole round earth is every way
Bound by gold chains about the feet of God.

The evils wrought by man, his lapses from reason when he detaches himself from human goodness, are the expressions of his baser self. The beast in him comes to the fore as an atavism that blocks the brotherhood of man and of nations. But a glimmer of hope breaks through the clouds of darkness that enshroud our universe; for the nobility of man shines forth time and again by precept and example. Human compassion glowed in the hearts of uncounted men and women who risked their lives to rescue Jews from the Nazi executioners. How can we reconcile the depravity of the Nazi in espousing mass murder with the humaneness of the Dutch and of the Danes? Nowhere, in no other period of history, has the ennobling quality of compassion been more clearly demonstrated than in the decency and heroism of thousands of men and women of France, Belgium, Norway, Italy—and Germany, too—who harbored and hid many a person intended for the furnaces of Buchenwald or the gas chambers of Auschwitz. Indeed, fallen angels have distorted man's image and purpose.

Shakespeare's Hamlet suggests man's condition, his glory and his almost-nothingness (II, 2):

. . . this goodly frame, the earth, seems to me a sterile promontory, this most excellent canopy, the air. . . . appears no other thing to me than a foul and pestilent congregation of vapours. What a piece of work is man! How noble in reason! How infinite in faculty, in form and moving! How express and admirable in action! How like an angel in apprehension! How like a god! The beauty of the world! The paragon of animals! And yet, to me, what is this quintessence of dust? Man delights not me,—no, nor woman neither, though by your smiling you seem to say so.

Shakespeare was only too aware of the baser side of "this quintessence of dust." His tragedies are replete with vengeance, murder, incest, hate and violence, and his Hamlet, again, asks the crucial question:

> What is man,
> If his chief good and market of his time
> Be but to sleep and feed? A beast, no
> more.

Seen not from the lofty perch of the theologian or the social scientist, but from the lowly pedestal of the endocrinologist, man has another side. The endocrinologist, too, asks "What is man?" except that he adds, "And woman, also?" For the endocrinologist is occupied with glandular and genetic influences that make man or make woman. An error in one or the other may so change physical makeup that the true identity of the individual is confused.

The factors that separate man from woman are tenuous. The endocrinologist recognizes true *hermaphrodites* with gonadal structures of both the male and female, and with external genitalia that are in a mixed state of development. He is aware of male and female pseudo-hermaphrodites; that is, persons with gonadal organs of one gender and incompletely differentiated external genitalia. He sees demi-females with failure of developmental growth of the ovaries, *Turner's syndrome*, and demi-males with very poor testicular development, frequently complicated by breast growth, *Klinefelter's syndrome*. And he finds males who think and act like females, and females whose aptitudes and attitudes are masculine, regardless of their sexual structures.

The normal female has twenty-two pairs of nonsex *chromosomes* or *autosomes* and an XX sex *chromosome complex*, resulting in the normal human chromosome compliment of forty six. The normal male has the same number of autosomes and an XY sex chromosome complex, for the total of forty-six. In the demi-females of Turner's syndrome, one-half of the XX complex is lost, so that they possess only forty-five chromosomes. In the demi-male of Klinefelter's syndrome, an extra X is present, so that the sex chromosome complex is XXY for a total of forty-seven chromosomes.

Some persons have all the appearances, instincts and drives of the female, yet harbor in their abdominal cavities testes instead of ovaries (the syndrome of feminizing testes). Their chromosomal pattern is similar to that of a male, but their bodies and minds belong to the female. Needless to say, these genetic anomalies may work havoc with the body form as well as with the personality, thus debasing the soul.

In a discussion of "What is man?" we must look back to our very beginnings, and ponder the written word: "So God created man in his own image, in the image of God created he him; male and female created he them" (Genesis 1:27). Metaphorically, we may assume that original man, Adam, was hermaphroditic. Such an assumption is quite permissible, for it is twenty-one verses after reporting the creation of man—how many millenia later I do not know—that we read

And the Lord God said, It is not good that the man should be alone: I will make him an help meet for him.   Genesis 2:18

In the history of human events is thus recorded man's earliest conception of the establishment of the sexes. Some of the most distinguished Hebrew writers, according to Selye, interpret the first chapters of Genesis as describing Adam as being of both sexes.

Hermaphroditus was a minor Greek divinity, half-man half-woman, the continuation of legend. But far from being the objects of worship and veneration, his unfortunate human successors became the objects of scorn and derision. The latter-day Greeks cast them into the sea. Legend has it that in Basle in 1474 even a cock was sentenced and burned at the stake for the heinous and unnatural crime of laying an egg. Thereabouts, too (Geneva, 1553), Michael Servetus, discoverer of pulmonary circulation, was burned at the stake.

Hermaphroditism has left an indelible imprint on the ladder of evolution, it seems, and its baneful legacy occasionally crops up in man. The different stages in the development of the individual reflect in a dimly vestigial manner some of the principal ancestral forms from which the species is descended. The earliest embryonic stages resembled the most remote ancestors. Now, the oprobrium has been extended to individuals who, save for their inability to reproduce their kind, have all the appearance and appurtenances of either maleness or femaleness.

Much may be done today to compensate for the glandular or genetic error. Removal of gonadal structures not in harmony with the instinctive drives of the individual, together with administration of replacement hormone therapy to develop the appropriate secondary sex characteristics, has met with considerable success. Also, surgery of the external genitalia is performed to enable the patient to conform with the laws of nature. Many such unfortunate individuals may be restored to semi-normalcy so that they may walk, head high and unbowed, with their spirits unbroken because of an error in development. Fate plays many tricks, and indeed there is a divinity that shapes our ends.

Some lay people and members of the clergy, as well as physicians, feel that interference, surgical or hormonal, with such individuals is against the will of God. Such arguments are not new and apply not alone to developmental abnormalities of man. When the Erie Canal was being built, there was strong opposition to it, even on religious grounds. Harry Emerson Fosdick told that at a Quaker meeting a solemn voice was heard. "If God had wanted a river to flow through the State of New York, He would have put one there." After a few moments of profound silence, another member rose and said simply, "And Jacob digged a well." An eloquent and sobering statement, something that reactionaries might well ponder.

Man is body and soul. Each influences the other. Man must rise above the common herd, the sheep, the beast in the field. Glandular and genetic disorders distort the image of man. When evolutionary reminders do crop up, they may, in a measure, be remedied. Notwithstanding the atavistic manifestations, man's animal instincts must forever be sublimated if our civilization is to endure.

GALL *Papaver somniferum*
They gave him vinegar to drink mingled with gall: Matthew 27:34

18

A Vessel Full of Vinegar

And the soldiers also mocked him, coming to him, and offering him
vinegar.   Luke 23:36

> *Why does "vinegar"—from the dawn of civiliza-*
> *tion a benefit to man as a medicine and as a*
> *condiment in preparing and preserving his food—*
> *connote unpleasantness?*

THE VINEGAR OF BIBLICAL DAYS actually was soured wine
and, although not particularly pleasant to the taste, refreshing. It
was the beverage of the tiller of the soil, the field hand, the soldier on
the march. In dry, arid climes it served as a prolonged thirst quencher;
in World War II, vinegar was added to the canteens of soldiers who
were deployed in areas where water was scarce, so that the supplies
would last longer.

Wine vinegar and apple-cider vinegar are relatively rich in potassium, a substance vitally important in the body's chemistry. Could it
be that the ancients unknowingly replenished potassium stores by its
ingestion? The cumulative experience of tribal man led him to assume
that such a drink also helped to lessen fatigue; recent researchers have
elucidated partially the role of potassium in energy exchange. Writing
in the second century, Galen—some authorities say he was a thousand
years ahead of his time—recommended for fatigue a concoction of
vinegar, honey, and water.

One of the early references to vinegar in the Bible is in the story of
Ruth:

And Boaz said unto her, At mealtime come thou hither, and eat of the
bread, and dip thy morsel in the vinegar. And . . . he reached her parched
corn, and she did eat, and was sufficed.   Ruth 2:14

The psalmist, however, regarded the vinegar drink as something

105

considerably less than ambrosial. When weary, troubled and in search of some comfort, he was chagrined by the offer of this refreshment. He cried out:

Reproach hath broken my heart; and I am full of heaviness
. . . and in my thirst they gave me vinegar to drink.   Psalm 69:20-21

Thus we observe the ambivalent regard in which vinegar was held—both as a delight and as a despair.

Vinegar has been employed in the healing arts throughout the centuries, for both internal and external uses. By 400 B.C. it was well established as a medicament, frequently prescribed by Hippocrates. The mildly acid property of vinegar evidently proved to be a bacterial inhibitor, for it was empirically employed in the treatment of wounds and bruises. Dioscorides (A.D. First Century) washed his hands in vinegar before undertaking a surgical procedure. The uses of vinegar have not altogether lessened with time and have become part of the folk medicine of our day.

In an age of unbelievable advancement in all branches of science, folk medicine often is discounted as superstitious nonsense. Yet many a simple remedy, which at first seems illogical and irrational, ultimately justifies its use. So with snakeroot, lowly weed, valued by Hindus as a soporific, and used by Gandhi to allay his anxieties during his political crises. What seemed a victory of mind over fact has been hailed as a "modern miracle" drug. Reserpine, the active alkaloid of snakeroot, was isolated from this weed and is the basis for one of the most important tranquilizing agents, Serpasil, also an effective suppressant of high blood pressure. From foxglove, a brew of which was imbibed by simple English country people with heart disease and dropsy, has come *digitalis*, the mainstay in today's management of the failing heart.

In the Middle Ages, an aromatic vinegar of Marseilles became known as *le vinaigre de quatre voleurs,* thought to be endowed with sovereign efficacy against plague and pestilence. According to the confession of four thieves who had plundered dead bodies during the plague at Marseilles, this preparation prevented them from contracting the disease while pursuing their nefarious trade.

Once it was fashionable for English physicians to carry a gold-headed cane as a symbol of their profession. During the eighteenth century, the head of the cane became known as a "vinaigrette," because the doctors put a tiny bottle of aromatic vinegar within the hollow knob and, when visiting the sick, inhaled the fumes to defend against contagion. Hogarth, famous artist and satirist, left to posterity an engraving which caricatured a group of well-known quacks of the day in sober consultation. Several are shown sniffing at their canes— "to each sagacious nose applied."

The uses of vinegar are legion. It is the douche universal. Mixed with clay, it is a poultice for swollen joints. It is a gargle for sore throat and an application for skin ailments (particularly the *dermatitis* that erupts beneath *orthopaedic* casts) a skin toughener, burn preventive and an after shampoo rinse to make the hair shine. And many a young mother knows that the pungent odor of the soiled diaper may be prevented by submerging it in a pail of water to which she has added vinegar: the vinegar neutralizes the alkaline ammonia.

In 1958, Dr. D.C. Jarvis brought renewed interest in vinegar to this country through his popular book, *Folk Medicine*. He concluded that the unusually rugged health of Vermonters is gained by their traditional mealtime drinking of a mixture of water and apple-cider vinegar (with honey, if desired). He reasoned that vinegar must be beneficial to man and beast, since he has repeatedly witnessed farm animals digging into and eating the soil on which mother of vinegar had been poured or spilled from an old keg. Dr. Jarvis believes, contrary to current medical opinion, that this old New England nostrum has withstood the test of time and is a preventive medicine or a remedy for countless ills. Its incorporation into the feed of horses and of cattle is said to enhance their fertility and to improve the sheen of the coat and the gloss of the hide.

In Biblical days, the analgesic benefits of wine-vinegar, when mixed with myrrh, frankincense, mandrake, or other herbal drugs such as gall, were well known. In the Gospels, Matthew and Mark differ about the drink proffered to Jesus; that is, whether it contained gall or myrrh. "And they gave him to drink, wine mingled with myrrh: but he received it not" (Mark 15:23). There is reason to believe that it may have been gall (*Papaver sommiferum*), an opium-poppy plant which thrives in the Holy Land, from which was derived a drug that eased suffering and induced sleep. Over the years, leading theologians from diverse branches of Christianity have joined other scholars in maintaining that this soothing liquid was offered to Jesus by the Daughters of Jerusalem, a small group of Jewish women dedicated to acts of charity and mercy. Deploring the Roman introduction of crucifixion, a deadly sin according to Jewish law, they prepared the anodyne to dull and stupefy those about to die by this inhumane form of execution. After Jesus was sentenced by Pontius Pilate, He was led away—

And there followed him a great company of people, and of women, which also bewailed and lamented him.

But Jesus turning unto them, said, Daughters of Jerusalem, weep not for me. . . . Luke 23:27-28

When the analgesic drink was proffered to Jesus to lessen his anguish, He refused it; He had resolved to endure the full measure of his suffering. "They gave him vinegar to drink, mingled with gall: and when he had tasted thereof, he would not drink" (Matthew 27:34). Finally, as the agonizing hours took their measure, Jesus said, "I thirst." It was then that one of the Roman soldiers, moved to compassion by the heroic endurance of their political prisoner, soaked a sponge in vinegar and held it up to Jesus. This time there was no additive of herbal drugs.

And straightway one of them ran, and took a spunge, and filled it with vinegar, and put it on a reed, and gave him to drink. Matthew 27:48

To quench their own thirst, the Roman soldiers kept a supply of the beverage within easy reach. Because all four Gospels agree, we may assume that the vinegar was at hand and that its usefulness was known well.

Some years ago, in California, a condemned man asked and received a pint of whiskey from Governor James Rolfe, Jr. The Governor had consulted with the chaplain of the legislature—Rabbi Norman Goldburg, now of Augusta, Georgia—who assured him that to offer the condemned a drink to mitigate suffering was traditional. Although the "righteous" flayed their Governor, one may wonder whether it is ever too late to dispense the milk of human kindness, even when the milk is alcoholic. Did not Jesus, in His final moments on the cross, taste of the wine of vinegar, to moisten His parched lips and to assuage His thirst?

Medicinal and restorative properties of soured acid wine have been known, then, since antiquity. This wine has served as an inexpensive and satisfying beverage, as a prolonged thirst-quencher, as a zesty condiment, as a vehicle by which the powers of herbal pain relievers are enhanced, and as a readily available and reportedly effective remedy for boundless ills. The progress of modern medicine has not dimmed the enthusiasm for vinegar as a household remedy for a host of illnesses of man and beast. The soured wine of the Bible has indeed enjoyed a useful, colorful and often bizarre role in the history of mankind.

Sarah, being passed the age of fertility, offers Hagar to Abraham.

19

Woman's Destiny

Now Abraham and Sarah were old and well stricken in age; and it ceased to be with Sarah after the manner of women   Genesis 18:11

Need the climacteric end a fruitful life?

ALL THE DAUGHTERS OF EVE experience three phases in their progression through womanhood: puberty, the reproductive years and the climacteric. The *menarche* outwardly manifests that pubescence is about to end and that the reproductive years are at hand. The *menopause*, the cessation of the menses, heralds the beginning of a change in the way of life, from fertility to the end of reproductive potential. Menstruation is regarded as a normal physiologic process—an imaginative gynecologist once called it "the womb weeping for the cast-off ovum"—but it is also a destructive process, frequently accompanied by toxic reactions and is truly Nature's curse on Eve.

The loss of fertility at the cessation of menses was recognized in antiquity. The Old Testament records that Sarah, wife of Abraham, conceived at an age so advanced that it had ceased to be with her "after the manner of women." She displayed the symptoms often linked to the change of life; cantankerous and irritable, she probably upbraided Abraham often. Her life had passed her by, and she had no proof of her womanhood to leave to posterity. She accused Abraham of being sterile and, challenging him, urged him to "go in unto my maid." Now it is not at all improbable that, in her menopausal state, Sarah urged with contempt, having every reason to believe him sterile. But Abraham accepted, "went in unto Hagar, and she conceived," (Genesis 16:4)

Thus was devised an early practical test to prove male fertility. Distasteful as it may seem today, it has not been discarded altogether. The realization of the importance of the male component in the study

111

of infertility still eludes some physicians, and often they neglect to evaluate the *seminal* status of the male partner.

When Hagar conceived, Sarah, vexed and hurt, in envy and despair sent the bondwoman away from her domicile. It was then that the Lord mercifully opened Sarah's womb: she bore a son and his name was Isaac. This birth is mentioned several times in the New Testament; Paul records it in this manner:

> And being not weak in faith, he [Abraham] considered not his own body now dead, when he was about an hundred years old, neither yet the deadness of Sarah's womb.   Romans 4:19

The resumption of *ovulation* in middle-aged women who have not menstruated in several years is encountered occasionally. *Uterine* bleeding, on the other hand, in women well past their menopause, does occur in the presence of hormone-producing ovarian tumors, and is noted also in hypertensives and in women with blood dyscrasia.

Several years ago, a woman of fifty-seven, who had migrated from Iraq to Israel, there ate fava beans for the first time. Her urine became tinged with red and was interpreted as menstrual flow. Now, fava beans contain a chemical component that, on ingestion, so sensitizes the red blood cells of certain Mediterranean people that they undergo dissolution. When, in the following spring, she came down with severe *hemolysis* and red-colored urine, she again blamed the Holy Land for its known miraculous effect on aged women. One may recall that Sarah, too, came from what is now Iraq as she journeyed from Ur of the Chaldees to the land of Canaan.

Sarah's attitude toward Hagar was a departure from the graciousness that characterized most of her life. In her impatience and anguish, she also showed her worst self in reproaching her husband:

> And Sarai said unto Abram, My wrong be upon thee: I have given my maid into thy bosom; and when she saw that she had conceived, I was despised in her eyes: the Lord judge between me and thee.   Genesis 16:5

Was Sarah's behavior part of the menopausal syndrome? The menopause is a rung of the ladder in a woman's progression through life, the climacteric, the change of life. During it, her balanced ovarian function declines and her menstrual flow ceases; she steps from reproductivity into middle age free from the responsibilities, the stresses, the hazards and the trials of childbirth—but at a price.

Because of her biologic constitution and the vicissitudes of her environment, the woman used to enter the climacteric with uneasy and uncertain tread. It was considered a time of introspection, of inventorying, and of soul-searching; she analyzed her limitations, her frustrations, her secret sorrows. For some it was anticipated as a period of boredom, of anxiety, of phobias and cancer fears, and even of waning romance. Unfortunately for some women it is still a period of emotional irritability, appearing at a stage in life when her nervous system may be unstable and vulnerable and when her declining ovarian activity provokes a general glandular imbalance. Little wonder, then, that the psychosexual upheaval that frequently was connected with this period brought with it a train of varied symptoms that one physician may have stamped as psychoneurotic and another as menopausal.

Such psychosomatic aspects of the menopause bring to mind a scene in Shakespeare's *Macbeth*, which lends substance to the concept that an emotional upheaval occurring during any given endocrine disorder is only an aggravation of preexisting neurotic tendencies. It is quite probable that Lady Macbeth became severely ill only when the environmental stresses were piled upon existing biologic deviations at her period of life. Macbeth is questioning the doctor about his wife (V, 3):

> *Macb.* How does your patient, doctor?
> *Doct.* Not so sick, my lord,
> As she is troubled with thick-coming fancies
> That keep her from her rest.
> *Macb.* Cure her of that.
> Canst thou not minister to a mind diseas'd,
> Pluck from the memory a rooted sorrow,
> Raze out the written troubles of the brain,
> And with some sweet oblivious antidote
> Cleanse the stuff'd bosom of that perilous stuff
> Which weighs upon the heart?
> *Doct.* Therein the patient
> Must minister to himself.

Now, as then, some physicians harbor this Doctor's attitude that "therein the patient must minister to himself." Furthermore, many thunder denunciations on all who administer hormones for the relief of the climacteric believing that it is a natural physiologic process. But, writes Dr. Minnie B. Goldberg of the University of California, "Why it should be more moral to treat the nervous symptoms of the menopause with barbiturates or tranquilizers than with natural substitutional products for a physiologic lack is a bit difficult to comprehend."

While it is true that the menopause is a physiologic process and represents a period of adjustment to a new hormonal *milieu intérieur*, why withhold measures that may make the transition smoother or prevent disabling pathologic processes be they psychologic, neuro-logic or metabolic? The fact is that many women may be restored from chronic invalidism to mental and physical health with the judicious use of steroid hormone therapy. We, as physicians, have within our power the means both to diagnose and to alleviate the distressing symptoms of the menopause. Those prepared to receive the lessons of endocrinology may offer these weary-laden women the hope that much can be done for them, that their gloom may be dispersed and their sufferings alleviated. We may share something of the optimism of Browning's *Rabbi Ben Ezra:*

> Grow old along with me!
> The best is yet to be,
> The last of life, for which the first was made:
> Our times are in His hand
> Who saith "A whole I planned,
> Youth shows but half; trust God: see all,
>   nor be afraid!"

That life begins at forty is a cliche, we all know; but for the vestal virgins, freed at forty from their service in the temples of Rome, life did begin so tardily, in a sense. The climacteric need not be the end of fruitful experience: if life does not begin in it, neither need it end. But if the advancing years are to be good, we must not deny those who require hormonal therapy for the troubles that beset them toward the "last of life."

The difficulties of the menopause—the imbalance of the *autonomic nervous system*, the psychogenic disorders, the metabolic disturbances— can continue, in mild to severe form, to the end of life. Many women cannot adjust to them; although their hormonal environment can be improved, they envision goals that must remain inaccessible. Their inner illuminations fade; their moments of exaltation give way to hours of melancholic gloom. In those who have staked everything on their femininity, the pathetic urgency to turn back the flight of time contributes to their crisis, for the life history and destiny of each woman depends to a great degree on the intensity and duration of her ovarian function. Of these matters Simone de Beauvoir has written well in her *The Second Sex*.

She who faces up to the responsibilities of her advancing years, who sets realistic goals, who minimizes her slights and hurts, real and imagined—she will grow old with grace and human worth. To her, the judicious use of hormones is of immeasurable help.

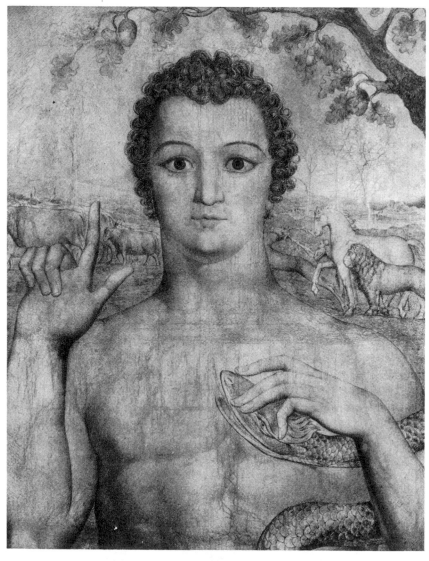

Adam – portrayed before the creation of Eve.

116

20

A Woman's Garment

The woman shall not wear that which pertaineth unto a man, neither shall
a man put on a woman's garment: for all that do so are abomination unto the
Lord thy God   Deuteronomy 22:5

Is the behavior of males who yield to an irrespressi-
ble urge to dress in woman's clothing conditioned by
environment or by glandular imbalance? A mani-
festation of distorted sexual values or of compulsion
neurosis?

OUR SOCIETY TENDS to emasculate the modern male; one may
read how frequently in the magazine section of the Sunday
paper. *Transvestism*, it is often said, is increasing, although any increase
may be more apparent than real. For transvestism was something of a
problem in Biblical days: Moses condemned it as an abomination to the
Lord, castigated transvestites, and forbade them to "enter into the
congregation of the Lord."

What another era regarded as willfull sinfulness, and soundly
denounced, a latter-day prophet of Israel, Sigmund Freud, dismissed as
merely an abnormality of behavior that is obsessive. The inquiring
eyes of modern science are taking another look at transvestism. To the
theories that try to explain the motivations that grip men to cross-
dress—environmental conditioning, glandular disorders, and psychic
disturbances—has been added a fourth dimension: possible defects in
the inherited chromosomal constitution.

Transvestism is a form of behavior in which a person has a
compulsive desire to dress in the clothes of the opposite sex. When
practiced in privacy, it is said to be a repressed and controlled
addiction; when flaunted in public, it is regarded as abnormal.
Occasionally, men participate in amateur shows as female inpersona-
tors. Certainly, such single instances do not consititute transvestism,

because they spring from no uncontrollable urge to gain erotic satisfaction. However, the male who repeatedly seeks such roles and, more particularly, the professional members of troupes are in many instances latent or true transvestites. In recent years, several dozen companies of female impersonators toured the nation's theaters and night clubs, playing to record audiences. What explanation can be offered for the increase in popularity of this form of entertainment? Of course, one recalls that in China and in Shakespeare's time men played all female roles for quite other reasons.

Havelock Ellis called this deviation "eonism," after the Chevalier d'Éon, famous French historical figure who was a transvestite. That unfortunate gentleman wrote with such excellence on history and political economy that he was sent on a diplomatic mission to Russia in 1755, where he dressed as a woman in order to win the confidence of the Empress. His disguise worked, and he secured a treaty favorable to France. Later, he held several high governmental positions and served as secretary to the French Ambassador to England, then as minister plenipotentiary. Wagers were placed that the Chevalier actually was a woman; but when he died, an autopsy revealed that he was undeniably a male. His name lives on; although d'Éon served his country faithfully, eonism has become synonymous with transvestism and a badge of dishonor.

Dr. Magnus Hirschfeld was first to use the term *transvestism*. It was his belief that the condition was an unusual sexual anomaly not necessarily related to homosexuality, and accordingly he recognized four types: heterosexual, homosexual, narcissistic and asexual. On the other hand, Alfred Kinsey's investigations led him to assume that this sexual deviation is a psychologically conditioned inclination, acquired after birth as a result of precise and specific environmental experiences; he disputed the theories of glandular causation and constitutional origin.

Historic reference to men who, by choice, behaved like women has appeared often in widely dispersed civilizations. Thirty centuries ago, this aberration was linked with religious customs in the worship of certain Babylonian deities. And further west among the Phoenicians, the Galli were sexual deviants who consecrated themselves to the worship of Astarte, a goddess akin to the Venus of the early Greeks.

In another part of the world, the Aztecs, for religious purposes, deliberately encouraged the Mujerado, who lost his position in society as a man and assumed female clothing and manners, for the sole reward of the high honor of being a religious consecrate. So, too, among the ancient Hebrews "consecrated ones," who actually were deviants or effeminate men, dwelt near the temples and were referred to as sodomites:

> And Judah did evil in the sight of the Lord, and they provoked him to jealousy with their sins. . . .
> And there were also sodomites in the land: and they did according to all the abominations of the nations which the Lord cast out before the children of Israel.   1 Kings 14:22, 24

In the original Hebrew, *kadesh*, literally "holy one," is the word which was translated "sodomite"—not exactly a complimentary substitute. In the Christian liturgy the resounding passage, "Holy, holy, holy, is the Lord of hosts: the whole earth is full of his glory" (Isaiah 6:3), is quite a familiar one. In the Hebrew, the word for Holy is *kadosh*. This passage is recited solemnly beginning in the words "Kadosh, kadosh, kadosh"—Holy, holy, holy. It is not difficult to surmise how the word kadesh evolved to describe someone set apart for holy purposes. In later years, this term was used to refer to "devotees of the fertility cult." Without this historic background, the association of the word kadosh (holy) with kadesh (sodomite) would appear wholly ludicrous. The reforming zeal of King Josiah ultimately prevailed and these abodes of immorality and heresy were destroyed (2 Kings 23:19).

If the reports are correct, the increase in transvestism in the United States and Europe is a phenomenon that strikingly illustrates the force of psychologic conditioning. This undesirable by-product of our way of life is a reflection of the mores and manners of the society in which we live. Unhappily, cross-dressing is not an uncommon occurrence among young men and women to whom it is known as "Hi-Drag." These frustrated persons find happiness when they are socializing with their own kind.

A few years ago, the newspapers carried a story of a scion of an aristocratic southern family who was murdered in his hideaway shack in the country. When found, he was dressed in woman's garb. Beside his battered head was a woman's shoe with a steel-pointed heel, and on one foot was its mate.

Several years ago, Dr. Christian Hamburger of Denmark was the recipient of world-wide publicity when he transformed a male transvestite into a female by surgery and hormone administration. Since that time, many physicians interested in problems of sex have been besieged by requests from discontented individuals to be transformed to the opposite sex. Within a few years after his report, Dr. Hamburger received such requests from three hundred and thirty-seven men and one hundred and eight women. In a more recent treatise on this subject, Dr. Jean Vague of Marseilles writes that the abnormal desire for sex transformation is widespread and endemic. The persons in this category, he feels, are not necessarily active, but all are at least passive homosexuals. The compulsive desire for sex transformation is an ancient malady, he states, and afflicted individuals harbor the belief that, but for some error in development, they actually belong to the opposite sex (see Chap. 29.)

One presumably intelligent college student, after studying the subject of chromosomes in his biology class, sought consultation with me requesting chromosome determinations. He earnestly believed that his was a female (XX) sex pattern, or at least a mixture of the male (XY) with the female (XX). This student argued that if such evidence could be brought forth, then his request for sex transformation would have valid support.

This young man's idea was ahead of his time; what he had surmised was prophetic. Only recently such a mosaic of XX/XY chromosomal sex patterns has been found in certain cases of defective sexual development. As our laws are constituted, sex transformation of normally developed individuals is illegal in many states and countries. However, the transformation of hermaphrodites and pseudohermaphrodites into the sex consonant with their psychic and emotional drives has been performed satisfactorily and within the bounds of legality.

With the American soldier who was the subject of much notoriety, Dr. Hamburger partially succeeded by castration and by the administration of female hormones. Though some degree of breast development may be induced and the pitch of the voice may be altered somewhat, the beard growth and the need for shaving cannot be eliminated except by meticulous electrolysis. Whether this deluded male is now happier in feminine guise as a "female" performer and entertainer remains a secret.

What should be the attitude of society, of the legal profession, of the psychiatrist and of the endocrinologist toward the transvestite with his compulsion for sex transformation? In quest for an answer, one may turn to the scriptures and find a partial answer:

He that is wounded in the stones . . . shall not enter into the congregation of the Lord.   Deuteronomy 23:1

In our age, should medical assistance ever be denied a transvestite? Therapy, psychiatric or endocrinologic, is difficult and, often, futile; nor is sex transformation through surgery a good answer to the problem. A part of the answer is early awareness, for as Milton wrote in *Paradise Regained:* "The childhood shows the man, / As morning shows the day," and as Wordsworth repeated after him: "The child is father of the man."

Yet attentive parents often observe peculiar behavior in their child or children, only then to conceal or ignore it. They should not ignore tendencies to cross-dress, but should seek help at once. For with proper guidance, and with conditioning before the tendency becomes the habit, much may be accomplished for this serious problem of behavior.

Eve tempts Adam in the Garden of Eden.

21

Sins Be As Scarlet

Come now, and let us reason together, saith the Lord: though your sins be as scarlet, they shall be as white as snow; though they be red like crimson, they shall be as wool.
Isaiah 1:18

Why, from antiquity until today, is sin equated with the color red, or crimson, or scarlet?

THE OLD AND THE NEW TESTAMENTS provide passages that equate shades of red with sinfulness. Isaiah refers to sins as *scarlet* and *red like crimson*. The repetition of a word-image—and the Old Testament abounds in it—is used by the prophet not only for effect but for emphasis. In mystical language, the New Testament Apostle John, dramatically reinforced the notion that sin wears a color. He, too, warned the people of:

. . . the great whore that sitteth upon many waters;
With whom the kings of the earth have committed fornication, and the inhabitants of the earth have been made drunk with the wine of her fornication.
. . . and I saw a woman sit upon a scarlet coloured beast, full of names of blasphemy, . . .
And the woman was arrayed in purple and scarlet colour.
Revelation 17:1-4

It is fascinating to examine the use of red shades to denote sin: vivid design in time's tapestry. Nathaniel Hawthorne's *The Scarlet Letter* tells the tragic story of Hester, a young woman who suffered the indignity of being branded with a scarlet "A"—the letter that marked her an adulteress. The "scarlet woman," the "red light district," "her crimson past" connote fully the relation of vivid red to sin, although ruby lips and rouged cheeks are today used with impunity not only to embellish but to attract, and the promise of feminine glamour not infrequently serves as a want ad.

Poets and artists have depended on red and its various shades to express sin; numerous paintings of debauchery depict females either scarlet-garbed or red-haired. Read the passages of Shakespeare's *The Rape of Lucrece* (lines 475–483) and give thought to the allusion subtly created when "lust-breathed Tarquin" is asked by the unwilling victim of his desire:

> But she with vehement prayers urgeth still
> Under what colour he commits this ill.
> Thus he replies: 'The colour in thy face,
> That even for anger makes the lily pale
> And the red rose blush at her own disgrace,
> Shall plead for me and tell my loving tale.
> Under that colour am I come to scale
> Thy never-conquer'd fort: the fault is thine,
> For those thine eyes betray thee unto mine.'

The question remains: Why should red, but not green or blue or yellow, be equated with sex and moral turpitude? The eye is drawn to other hues, but only a red is coupled with sin. Green is a reminder of earth's rebirth in the spring, and implies hope; gold indicates warmth and richness; the sky and ocean are blue to the eye, and suggest harmony. In nature, there is a minimum of red except for fruit, flowers, fire, and fall's spent leaves. And in our culture even though white is thought correct for a bridal gown, again history reports that red once was popular. The custom was not lasting because, in the human mind is ingrained a feeling that white expresses purity and virginity while red does not.

Why red's wicked reputation among colors? The Old Testament tells us that man's downfall, and what is termed "original sin," took place in the Garden of Eden; Adam and Eve were cast from Paradise because they disobeyed God and ate of the forbidden fruit, generally pictured as a red apple. The paintings of such masters as Titian and Rubens display this red fruit; the apple, althouth not specified in Genesis, became the fruit of temptation. Milton named it, in *Paradise Lost*, as "fair apples," described previously in the poem as "ruddy and gold." Plainly, the fruit's color did not cause it to be attached to evil; instead, it was probably selected because a "sinful shade" emphasized a sinful deed, and the apple suited all requirements.

Another theory concerns the shedding of blood during sacrifice, with which pagans sought to appease their gods and which the ancient Hebrews were enjoined to practice by Jehovah to win his forgiveness of sins. Sacrifice was a ritual, and the Hebrews believed that their sins were shed from them as an animal's blood drained away after the slaughtering; an unblemished red heifer was their special offering. Christians find their answer in Christ's blood, which was offered, during the crucifixion, as the supreme sacrifice for the atonement of all men's sins. By its blood offering, the sacrifice has a relation, direct or indirect, to sin.

A Biblical verse, like any remark taken out of context, may invite misunderstanding. But Isaiah's words regarding sin follow seventeen verses of condemnation of his people. Judah had many vices, yet Isaiah seemed most wrathful toward the nation's lack of sexual morality and rebuked them, saying:

Ah sinful nation, a people laden with iniquity, a seed of evildoers, children that are corrupters. . . .
Except the Lord of hosts had left unto us a very small remnant, we should have been as Sodom, and we should have been like unto Gomorrah.
Hear the word of the Lord, ye rulers of Sodom: give ear unto the law of our God, ye people of Gomorrah. . . .
Your hands are full of blood.
How is the faithful city become an harlot!   Isaiah 1:4, 9-10, 15, 21

The great prophet gave particular attention to sins of the flesh in these verses. He selected scarlet, red, and crimson as symbolic of immorality, warning that his people had been spared the fate of Sodom because only "a very small remnant" refrained from the corruption that brought its destruction. Sin's color was thus defined and eloquently expressed by Isaiah, in the Eighth Century B.C.

The identification of sin with red could date back to times much earlier than Isaiah's: the Mosaic laws proclaim a menstruating woman unclean and sexual intercourse during menstruation sinful. It is possible that the symbolism of red can be traced back to an even earlier period. Our oldest civilizations flourished in India, where the macaque (a short-tailed monkey) is indigenous, and not infrequently revered. The sexual habits of the macaque were in all probability closely observed. Perhaps it is in the study of the sex skin changes in these primates that an answer to the question may be found. At the time when the ovary prepares to extrude the ovum or egg, the genital zone of the macaque becomes turgid and takes on a brilliant red color. The period of greatest sexual receptivity in the female macaque is reached during this period of turgescence and "redness" of the sex skin. Flaunting her nakedness, she sports her colors; her "redness" is her open invitation to mating.

Such terms as "red light" and "the scarlet woman" are profoundly symbolic because vestiges of our most primitive impulses crop up from time to time. As man evolved, these blatant advertisements, veritable neon signs, were no longer necessary to the highest species, man being moved by more subtle appeals. In the phylogenetic development of man, the female homo sapiens apparently lost the readily visible color changes of the sex skin inherent in the macaque. Yet today, the eyes of science have discovered that indeed woman has retained significant color changes of the perineum. Greatly modified, the sex skin of the adult female still retains the atavistic red. In the study of gynecologic disorders and during pregnancy, colors of the genitalia, varying from vivid red to purple, can be made visible by illumination with an ultraviolet light.

In the light of all of these considerations, we should not be surprised that sex, sin and scarlet have been interwoven in the fabric of our literature and mores. It was no mere accident that Isaiah observed: "though your sins be as scarlet . . . though they be red like crimson. . . ." (1:18).

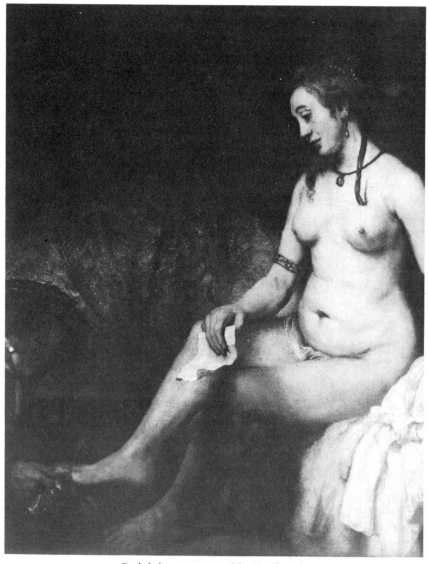

Bathsheba, as portrayed by Rembrandt.

128

22

No Breasts Hath She

We have a little sister, and she hath no breasts: what shall we do for our sister in the day when she shall be spoken for?

If she be a wall, we will build upon her a palace of silver: and if she be a door, we enclose her with boards of cedar.   Song of Solomon 8:8–9

Is the little sister's condition less a handicap today, or more? Are our walls stouter, our doors more open?

BLESS ME, Socrates said looking around in the market where all that any Athenian wanted lay piled in profusion, "What a lot of things a man can do without." One of the things that we of this culture can *not* do without is apparently, the female breast.

We are a nation of breast-worshipers. In art and literature, in the theater and the movies, on television and in advertising, we glorify the female mammary glands. For a woman, the full development of her bosom is a needful thing. She knows that men consider well-formed breasts the mark of beauty and of womanhood, and even equate them, erroneously, with sexual prowess. In our day, we have seen a great resurgence of the esteem of the female breast as a symbol of sex, femininity and abundance.

Yet has it not been so always? With and without the singing of birds and the voice of the turtle dove in the land, poets have sung with more charm, perhaps, than innocence:

Thy two breasts are like two young roes that are twins, which feed among the lilies.

Until the day break, and the shadows flee away, I will get me to the mountain of myrrh, and to the hill of frankincense.

Song of Solomon 4:5–6

Adequate maturation of the breasts was an important factor in the

129

marriage marts. Small wonder, then, that the brothers of the little sister were worried. One must feel the urgency of their question: "What shall we do for our sister in the day when she shall be spoken for?"

Was the sister suffering from sexual infantilism or merely from the absence of the growth of her breasts? How were her brothers to meet the competition in the marketplace? Her lack had perhaps given her such feelings of inferiority that she had become asocial, introverted, unapproachable: an impenetrable wall. If so, her brothers would endow her handsomely, would "build upon her a palace of silver." On the other hand, if in order to compensate for her wants and to prove her femininity she had become too approachable, even promiscuous— a hospitable door through which all could enter—they would chaperone and confine her, would "enclose her with boards of cedar."

This interpretation of what probably beset the little sister and her brothers followed my study of two young women with sexual infantilism whom I saw in consultation. The first was twenty-three years old, shy and retiring; because she was ashamed of her nakedness, she had refused an offer of marriage. Substitutional therapy, with cyclic use of estrogens over a two-year period, changed her personality to that of an outgoing person and resolved her problem. She is happily married and is most appreciative of hormone therapy, which she has continued.

The second young woman, of about the same age, was bold and brazen; her every action was an effort to show how womanly she could be. I was scandalized to find her trademark tatooed on the base of what we may call, I suppose, her escutcheon: "Pay as you enter." Hers, surely, was a device of overcompensation.

Lack of breast development may derive from one of three causes: delayed pubescence, ovarian failure, or target-gland failure—failure of the breasts to respond to the hormones produced by the ovaries, the estrogens. For delayed pubescence, time and expectant waiting are all that is necessary, although breast maturation may be hastened by the administration of hormones; and such hastening is valuable when anxiety may lead to psychic problems. For ovarian failure, the cyclic administration of estrogens will result, usually, in excellent breast growth. For target-gland failure, often encountered, the addition of hormones usually proves, unfortunately, valueless. Because the breast tissues fail to respond to the stimulus of endogenous hormones, they also fail to respond, in almost all cases, to exogenous hormones. One may speculate into which one of the three categories the "little sister" falls, in the Song of Solomon.

Archaeologists continue to unearth statues from ancient civilizations that depict women with voluptuous breasts. In the ancient cultures of India, Egypt, and Babylon, prominent breasts were accepted for what they appeared to be, an erotic fixture. The Phoenician goddess of fertility and of sexual love, Astarte, is depicted as having many breasts. Women in all periods of our civilization have been conscious of the well-developed bosom. The ancient Jews had an appreciation of the breasts that was closer to hearth and home—earthy as it was. Proverbs exhorts a husband to:

... rejoice with the wife of thy youth.
Let her be as the loving hind and pleasant roe; let her breasts satisfy thee at all times; and be thou ravished always with her love.   Proverbs 5:18-19

Nor was the life-giving sustenance furnished by the lactating breast disregarded. Ashley Montagu believes that the Psalmist, in unconscious reverberation, almost certainly had this in mind when he wrote the words, "I lift up mine eyes unto the hills, from whence cometh my help [sustenance]," 121:1.

But in Solomon's Song the human breast is glorified. In eight short chapters the subject is sung eight times without sham or shame.

A bundle of myrrh is my well-beloved unto me; he shall lie all night betwixt my breasts.   Song of Solomon 1:13

The Song has been termed by some as pagan and lewd. Such pious disapproval of a theme written with delicacy and tenderness nearly resulted in exclusion of this classic of religious literature from the Bible. Even at the close of the nineteenth century, the Reverend E. P. Eddruff, Prebendary of Salisbury Cathedral, adominished that "such a book as the Song of Solomon may not be fitted for public reading in a mixed congregation, or even in private reading by the impure of heart." Despite such protestations, the Song will always remain a paean to love, in praise of the body beautiful, and a timeless tribute to womanhood.

Nor was it very different in Imperial Rome when Aulus Gellius said:

And do you suppose that nature has given bosoms to women only to add to their beauty—more for the sake of ornament than for the purpose of nourishing children? Because some women believe this, they unnaturally endeavor to dry up and extinguish that sacred fountain of the body, the natural nourishment of man, with great hazard, turning and corrupting the channel of their milk, lest it should render the distinction of their beauty less marked.

What a familiar bell is rung by this commentary written in the second century! *Nihil novum est.*

The veneration of the female breast is nothing new. Man has always been enthralled, it seems, by the sight of the shapely breast. Women throughout history have been aware of the allure to men of reticent exposure of the subtly clothed breast. The plunging neckline may not be equated with plunging morals, but certainly it is an integral part of a coquettish pattern, of flirtation, of invitation to attention. The extent to which a woman is willing to reveal, or to emphasize, her breasts is also a measure of her conscious sexuality. While there is no sexual symbolism in the nakedly displayed bosom of the native African woman, there is considerable sexual identification with the purposefully low-cut revealing gown of the fully clothed woman. The young matron or teenager with a tightly fitting sweater covering an uplift bra or bare breasts is merely exaggerating her desirability and sometimes her availability. Feminine curves have been appreciated since Adam beheld Eve. In an inconstant world of continuous and spectacular change, one thing remains constant, and that is the unchanging appreciation by civilized man of the bosom as a symbol of fertility, bounty and beauty.

The sick woman touching the hem of Jesus' garment.

23

Thy Faith Can Make Thee Whole

And a woman having an issue of blood twelve years, which had spent all her living upon physicians, neither could be healed of any,

Came behind him, and touched the border of his garment: and immediately her issue of blood stanched.   Luke 8:43-44

Was the woman with "an issue of blood" suffering from a psychosomatic disorder? And was she healed by faith?

THE RELATIONSHIP between psychic and physical expression of human behavior lies in the realm of body and soul. Here mystery and illness are joined, and the cure of sickness takes many forms. The laying on of hands, an accepted form of therapy in early Christian times, was revived in England during the reign of Edward the Confessor; and Charles II later set aside one day each year to touch those affliced with scrofula, "the King's disease." The throngs came to London; the King touched; and those who remained ill "lacked faith."

Yet faith can cure. The crutches that line the walls of the shrine at Sainte Ann de Beaupré, in Montmorency, Canada, bear witness to the cures rendered by faith. That multitudes journey from all the countries of the earth to the shrine of Lourdes, in France, means that some are healed, else the procession of suppliants would cease.

Two thousand years ago, the Holy Land was overrun by the Roman conquerors. A stubborn and stiffnecked people, the Hebrews suffered in silence heavy taxes and severe restrictions. Powerless to overthrow their oppressive yoke, they were frustrated and soul-sick. Although as they yearned for salvation they gave lip-service to Rome, their loyalty was to God, King of the Universe. It is not unnatural that during the ministry of Jesus of Nazareth, when the atmosphere was charged with peaceful disobedience, illness abounded, both organic and psychosomatic. Today we readily accept the fact that many cases of migraine headaches, of mucous diarrhea, of hives, rashes and welts, and of localized spotty loss of head hair and even of all body hair, are physical manifestations of some deep-rooted emotional conflict; that is, that they are psychosomatic. Functional uterine bleeding, though readily explained as a disturbance of pituitary-ovarian balance, is nevertheless frequently emotional or psychogenic, a psychosomatic disorder; prolonged bleeding often follows severe fright or calamity. Psychosomatic disturbances play a role in uterine bleeding greater than that we have been wont to credit.

An inkling of such is suggested by the woman cured when she touched Jesus' garment. To her, He said: "Daughter, be of good comfort: thy faith hath made thee whole; go in peace" (Luke 8:48) His ability to suffuse her being with such faith is a miracle that transcends the miracle of the arrest of bleeding within a few hours by today's potent hormonal preparations, such as *progesterone*. But even with these, the physician may cure, or he may add insult to injury. For if he wants confidence in his medication or his ability, if he neglects rapport with his patient, he may become an *iatrogenic* agent, just as certain pharmaceutical drugs may induce or compound a disease state, and thereby encourage his patients to develop hostility to the entire medical profession.

Mark, telling the same story that Luke told, bluntly took to task the doctors of his day when he described the woman as having "suffered many things of many physicians" (5:26). Clearly, he implied that she had suffered at their hands many more things than need be.

Human relationships, particularly those between doctor and patient, enter every medical situation. Like the lower animals, man fears and frets; unlike them, he has intellect and conscience, suffers forebodings and frightful imaginings, fluctuates in his emotional responses, and holds a wavering grasp on security. In one so sensitive occur reverberations that react on soma and psyche, body and soul; hence psychologic factors may as easily create as ameliorate a climate of preoccupation with infirmity. Therefore, the physician cannot study man in the biologic sense alone, for man's soul must be so nurtured that his body may function harmoniously in all its parts. The higher centers of the brain temper the activity of the pituitary glands, and the endocrines respond to the nervous system.

All of medicine is in part psychosomatic, for emotional factors influence physical behavior. The anxious suspicious person often suffers from dyspepsia; he "thinks" with his stomach. In the light of this concept, we may appreciate obesities in maladjusted persons, *exophthalmic goiter* in those subjected to repeated psychic trauma, menstrual disorders in women who experience stressful episodes, and *anorexia nervosa* in tormented young women. As Shakespeare's King Lear observed (II, 4):

> we are not ourselves
> When nature, being oppress'd, commands the mind
> To suffer with the body.

Perhaps psychotherapy, faith healing and the frequent beneficial effects that follow inadequate or inert therapy may take on new significance for us. Just as sorrow and pain may cause illness, and happiness and pleasure make for good health, so healing and cure do not come always from skill or from specifics. Faith, hope and charity ("but the greatest of these . . .") in an infusion of lovingkindness may do much more. Charity usually translated "love" (agape) is the expression of righteousness, the obligation of the good man, man's act of reverence for man and of compassionate respect for him. Charity is the expression of a noble soul.

And charity (love) is a great healer. In the management of illness that links psyche and soma, the general practitioner and specialist, the endocrinologist and psychiatrist, the psychotherapist and the minister meet on common ground. Christ spoke an eternal truth when he told the woman: "thy faith hath made thee whole; go in peace."

King David in old age – from a 19th century engraving.

24

When Desire Shall Fail

Now king David was old and stricken in years; and they covered him with clothes, but he gat no heat. 1 Kings 1:1

Was the aging King David fairly tested? Did the struggle within him of righteousness against lust, and worse, abet his aging?

FROM THE AGE OF FIFTY King David had no rest from misfortune and emotional turmoil. At seventy, he was so spent that he could lead his people no longer. Was he suffering from circulatory failure, severe *anemia, hypothyroidism,* or from general apathy and decrepitude? Rumblings were abroad, rumor raced through the kingdom that the King was through, and a Pretender laid claim to the throne.

The criteria that determined the King's loss of usefulness to his state seem strange to us. Was the fact that he "gat no heat" when covered with clothes a valid test of his fitness for leadership? The clinical observation was not strong enough to force his abdication; a more exacting test was needed; and the Israelites were prone to equate sexual prowess with virility and strength.

Wherefore his servants said unto him, Let there be sought for my lord the king a young virgin: and let her stand before the king, and let her cherish him, and let her lie in thy bosom, that my lord the king may get heat.

So they sought for a fair damsel throughout all the coasts of Israel, and found Abishag a Shunammite, and brought her to the king.

And the damsel was very fair, and cherished the king, and ministered to him: but the king knew her not. 1 Kings 1:2-4

Oh what pride must have been in the hearts of Abishag's parents when their daughter was chosen from all Israel to lie with the King! Although the origin of this sanctioned privilege is lost in antiquity, the

139

claim of a prince continued through the middle ages. *Le droit du seigneur* could not be denied the lord of a domain, a baron, or the prince of a petty principality. The custom was extended to rights on the wedding night of the bride, and *droit de noce* was exacted from a subjugated people.

"When Abishag tried to arouse the King, he still "gat no heat" and so failed the test. One can imagine her proud and anxious parents awaiting her return, their meeting, and the disillusion and dismay of all three. Word of the King's loss of virility spread throughout the kingdom, and his leadership was in doubt. Bath-sheba confronted the King to ensure that he declare her son by him, Solomon, as successor. And Solomon grew from strength to strength, and it is said of him that he had a thousand wives.

We may wonder whether David was in the throes of the *male climacteric,* akin to the female change of life. Although students of glandular physiology have not been unanimous that the male climacteric exists, proof that it does is strong. We know today that the climacteric occurs in both sexes, but that it affects only a small proportion of men. With advancing years, the endocrine output lessens to insufficiency. Testicular decline is great in some, less in others. But the activity of the adrenals persists at moderately normal levels in all; and when adrenal activity is greater than testicular, then *catabolism* overbalances *anabolism,* and decline follows inevitably.

Environmental and emotional factors play important roles in and can hasten senescence. An early indication is loss of virility or potentia. Prominent symptoms are psychosexual upheaval, insommia, loss of concentration, irritability and melancholia. At this stage, men often become antisocial, and many lose confidence in their abilities. When psychogenic factors do not greatly overshadow the declining hormonal function of the testes, augmentive therapy, with androgens, has been most helpful in decreasing physical and mental fatigability, restoring vitality, and markedly improving general well-being.

None will dispute David's greatness as a king. When a lad, he was gifted in playing the lyre; he exhibited unusual courage as a humble shepherd who slew both lion and bear to protect his father's flocks. A favorite story describes his skill and bravery in killing Goliath, the giant, whom he faced alone, armed with only a slingshot. His sweet songs soothed the ill King Saul, who was to become obsessed by jealousy of him. Later, David was crowned king of Israel; but after a long and hard-fought civil war waged against Saul's house, he emerged triumphant to reign over all Israel. His armies succeeded in conquering a feared and hated foe, the Philistines. Displaying adeptness in every way, he was a shrewd military leader, organizer and administrator. His nature was complex—a common denominator of most geniuses. He affords us a study in personality contrasts: humble but majestic; a sensitive psalmist yet a courageous warrior.

But King David had problems born of the struggle within him of opposing instincts. He was a man who cherished a specially close contact with God; from his simple faith had grown a strong, unbending conscience. And he was a man of great passion as well, having taken under the law, which also permitted him ten concubines, a number of wives. Within him, his conscience was now to struggle with his passion become lust, and worse.

At fifty, he succumbed to a temptation that was to bring sore trouble. At this age, we realize, a man may be tempted to prove his virility simply because he has less of it, because his sexuality has diminished. It is a time of life when physical, mental, and emotional upsets are not endured easily. Resistance is low; a surge of restlessness, of loneliness, is a constant threat. David had returned to his palace, after numerous victories, for relaxation well earned. Restive, he

arose from off his bed, and walked upon the roof of the king's house: and from the roof he saw a woman washing herself; and the woman was very beautiful to look upon.   2 Samuel 11:2

She was Bath-sheba, wife of Uriah, one of David's brave and loyal captains.

A sudden desire subdued David's sense of righteousness. Impulsively, he sent for her. Doubtless she was flattered to be summoned by her king. When she discovered herself pregnant, David lost no time in bringing her husband home from the battle, expecting, thereby, to conceal his adultery. But Uriah, despite all persuasion, refused to enter his house while Israel's army suffered on the grim field of battle. Sending Uriah back to the fighting, David had him placed in a position in which death was inescapable, and, after the days of mourning, he took Bath-sheba to be his wife.

The effect of this tragic affair on a sensitive, God-loving man who had sought to live in righteousness cannot be overestimated. David had

141

lost contact with his Lord, and no longer understood himself. Men of his character are prone to expect trouble; they even invite it as penance to soothe their feelings of guilt.

> Wherefore hast thou despised the commandment of the Lord, to do evil in his sight? thou hast killed Uriah the Hittite with the sword, and hast taken his wife to be thy wife . . .
> Now therefore the sword shall never depart from thine house . . .
> Thus saith the Lord, Behold, I will raise up evil against thee.
>
> 2 Samuel 12:9-11

David had expected grim punishment, and Nathan's unstill voice foreshadowed his soul's agony. He suffered one misfortune after another, and his personal concerns gave him harsher trial than many overwhelming national problems. Certain that his woes were a sure sign of God's wrath, the once-majestic king aged beyond his years. As his feelings of guilt played havoc with his well-being, so he evidenced signs and symptoms of the male climacteric. The sight of Abishag surely stirred in him old memories; but she could not arouse him, and he failed the test.

A man's strength comes from proper endocrine functioning and peace of mind. Because Israel required a strong king, it accepted as the symptom of infirmity a lack of sexual desire. Yet no yardstick has been devised that equates a man's age with his ability properly to grapple with his duties and responsibility, whether of state, profession, or business. The test of the ancient Hebrews, however exacting, was and is fallible.

Noah, like others of the antediluvian era, was reputed to have lived to a great age.

25

Seven Ages

Remember now thy Creator in the days of thy youth, while the evil days come not, nor the years draw nigh, when thou shalt say, I have no pleasure in them;

While the sun, or the light, or the moon, or the stars, be not darkened, nor the clouds return after the rain:

In the day when the keepers of the house shall tremble, and the strong men shall bow themselves, and the grinders cease because they are few, and those that look out of the windows be darkened,

And the doors shall be shut in the streets, when the sound of the grinding is low, and he shall rise up at the voice of the bird, and all the daughters of musick shall be brought low;

Also when they shall be afraid of that which is high, and fears shall be in the way, and the almond tree shall flourish, and the grasshopper shall be a burden, and desire shall fail . . .

Or ever the silver cord be loosed, or the golden bowl be broken, or the pitcher be broken at the fountain, or the wheel broken at the cistern.

Then shall the dust return to the earth as it was: and the spirit shall return unto God who gave it.

Vanity of vanities, saith the preacher; all is vanity. Ecclesiastes 12:1-8

Has the stress of our times, the way of our lives, aged man? Toward the aged, what should society's attitude be?

MAN ATTAINED UNBELIEVABLE AGE in the antediluvian era: Methuselah lived 969 years, Noah 950. The life-span in the postdiluvian era is comparable to our own: Moses died at 120, and King David lived out threescore years and ten. What has happened to the "nucleic acid moiety," or to the aging process, that has brought about this radical change? Was it a change in the nature of the foodstuffs that sustained man, or new unaccustomed viruses that afflicted him? Or was it—let us remember that the priest Berossos, writing in Babylonia in the Third Century B.C., totaled the reigns of three preflood kings at 68,400 years—that the Biblical "year" was much shorter than ours, or that the geneaologies were composed before man had developed an exact chronology and felt the need to measure time with precision?

At the beginning of the eighteenth century, the average life span in the civilized world, although many reached a ripe old age, was not more than thirty-five years, and at the beginning of the twentieth century, in the United States, was only forty-nine years. Today, it is seventy-two years. The "three score and ten" of Biblical promise has become a reality for more people now than ever before. Whereas only four per cent of our population reached the age of sixty in 1900, more than nine per cent are sixty-five or older today.

The process of aging, in all probability, has ever been the same. Centuries apart, two poet-philosophers, Koheleth-Ecclesiastes and Shakespeare, described advancing age after the same fashion. To compare the style of Ecclesiastes, cloaked in mystery of language and metaphor, with the style of Shakespeare, clearer to us and relatively simpler, some eighteen centuries later is fascinating. In *The Comedy of Errors* (V, 1), Aegeon remarks the attrition of his aging;

> Though now this grained face of mine be hid
> In sap-consuming winter's drizzled snow,
> And all the conduits of my blood froze up,
> Yet hath my night of life some memory,
> My wasting lamps some fading glimmer left,
> My dull deaf ears a little use to hear. . . .

In the more sophisticated *As You Like It* (II, 7) the caustic, melancholy Jacques sets forth the human condition:

> All the world's a stage,
> And all the men and women merely players:
> They have their exits and their entrances;
> And one man in his time plays many parts,
> His acts being seven ages. . . .

Then he describes each age in turn—the infant "Mewling and puking in the nurse's arms;" the boy "creeping like snail / Unwillingly to school;" the lover, "Sighing like a furnace;" the soldier / "Seeking the bubble reputation / Even in the cannon's mouth;" the justice / "In fair round belly with good capon lin'd," . . .

The sixth age shifts
Into the lean and slipper'd pantaloon,
With spectacles on nose and pouch on side,
His youthful hose, well sav'd, a world too wide
For his shrunk shank; and his big manly voice,
Turning again toward childish treble, pipes
And whistles in his sound. Last scene of all,
That ends this strange eventful history,
Is second childishness and mere oblivion,
Sans teeth, sans eyes, sans taste, sans everything.

The aging process is universal. As the perceptive Shakespeare captured it for his lively audiences, he seems to have paraphrased many of the thoughts and the symbols of Koheleth-Ecclesiastes:

grinders cease because they are few—*sans teeth*
those that look out of the windows be darkened—*sans eyes*
sound of the grinding is low—*my dull deaf ears*
daughters of musick shall be brought low—*childish treble*
almond tree shall flourish—*face of mine be hid in snow*
desire shall fail—*night of life some memory*
wheel broken at the cistern—*conduits of my blood froze up*

For many centuries scholars have sought to unravel the mystery of Koheleth's description of that time of man's sojourn on earth when his life ceases to be a joy, when his faculties decline and his strength fails. Koheleth wrote of the aged with compassion, and in the twelfth chapter he has given us a remarkable exposition of the rigors of aging and of its inevitable toll. In so doing, he touched on several medical fields, of which we believe little was known. Linking antiquity to the present, his observations are pertinent:

"The clouds return after the rain" (2). Here the poet-clinician recognizes the mental and emotional changes associated with aging: depression, disappointment, dreary expectations.

"The keepers of the house shall tremble" (3). Variously interpreted, this metaphor may refer to trembling hands or to the jerky, gasping heaving of the chest, which houses the vital organs.

"And the strong men shall bow themselves" (3). The muscles, cartilage and bones degenerate, the legs bow, the shoulders stoop, perhaps with arthritis.

"And he shall rise up at the voice of the bird" (4). Almost all old people wake and arise early in the morning.

"They shall be afraid of that which is high, and fears shall be in the way"

(5). Fear, particularly of heights, and apprehension often accompany the infirmities of old age.

"Or ever the silver cord be loosed, or the gold bowl be broken" (6). In keeping with the anatomical allegory so precisely drawn, the silver cord becomes the spinal column, weakened by the demineralization of the bones (osteoporosis); and the broken bowl denotes the deterioration, through hemorrhage or softening, of the brain in its cranial vault.

"The pitcher broken at the foutain" (6). The broken pitcher denotes the urinary incontinence and the troublesome prostate gland common in aged men.

"The wheel broken at the cistern" (6). Here is a graphic metaphor of cardiac failure: the heart pump is affected by coronary thrombosis.

What is aging? It is the wear and tear of tissues throughout the body. The process starts, actually, with one's first breath, surely with the first lusty cry at birth. Building processes predominate from birth until late puberty; then, for a varying number of years, the forces that build (anabolism) and those that destroy (catabolism) reach some sort of equilibrium, before the rigors of aging begin. Insulin and growth and gonadal hormones contribute to anabolism, and certain hormones of the adrenal contribute to catabolism. When the anabolic gonadal function (ovarian or testicular) declines, breakdown of tissue proceeds at a more rapid rate than build-up. As aging depends on the hormonal chemistry of the body, so it depends on genetic endowment, also.

Sex desire in healthy persons parallels gonadal function; hence the allusion in Ecclesiastes is in accord with physiological principles. Shakespeare's Poins makes the point more graphically and realistically: "Is it not strange that desire should so many years outlive performance?" (II *Henry IV,* II, 4). Lack of sexual performance is indeed one of the indices that aging is upon us.

Yet the calendar is a poor index of a person's age. Too often persons are forced to retire while still mentally and physically alert, and in many of them, their stimulation and self-confidence taken away, their will to live ebbs, and they die before their time. Countless "old" people, even with physical limitations, live vibrant useful lives— meeting the challenges of each day, maintaining their interests and talents, living one day at a time, without regrets for yesterday's mistakes or anxieties about tomorrow's: "for the morrow shall take thought for the things of itself" (Matthew 6:34). In many, facing the sunset of their existence, the spark of youth persists; they prove the fallacy of judging competence by a fixed scale of years.

Society is the beneficiary of untold wealth bequeathed to it by men considered long past their prime, as Longfellow makes clear in his *Morituri Salutamus*:

> It is too late! Ah, nothing is too late
> Till the tired heart shall cease to palpitate.
> Cato learned Greek at eighty; Sophocles
> Wrote his grand *Oedipus,* and Simonides
> Bore off the prize of verse from his compeers,
> When each had numbered more than four-score years, . . .
> Chaucer, at Woodstock with the nightingales,
> At sixty wrote the *Canterbury Tales;*
> Goethe at Weimar, toiling to the last,
> Completed *Faust* when eighty years were past.
> These are indeed exceptions; but they show
> How far the gulf-stream of our youth may flow
> Into the arctic regions of our lives. . . .
> For age is opportunity no less
> Than youth itself, though in another dress, . . .

What of the attitude of modern society toward the aged? Is it one of responsible acceptance, of wise understanding, of social usefulness? Or is it evasive, disrespectful, socially destructive?

The scientific aspects of aging receive more attention than ever before, and the social, political and economic problems of the aged population currently are in the national forum, especially medical care for the aged. Inasmuch as the population of senior citizens is expanding phenomenally, our society must shape its resources to meet and to ameliorate their plight. While the increase in population is owing to the great advances in the medical and biological sciences during the past century, solutions to the problems that the increase creates must involve not only expanding medical care but also attending to a matrix of social, economic, and environmental facts.

Aged human beings have fundamentally the same problems around the world. They require the same commodities: food, shelter, clothing. But, in whatever culture, they also require another kind of sustenance—as Dr. David Sherman, past president of the American Geriatric Society, has stated, "emotional sustenance and self-esteem."

> How dull it is to pause, to make an end,
> To rust unburnished, not to shine in use!

said the poet. To be active usefully and responsibly, to be wanted and valued—these are the best tonics for the boredom and frustration of old age in our society.

In one way or another, the problem of the aged belongs to each individual: the aged are genuinely ours, as we must some day be numbered of them. We must create opportunities for their work and their play, for their answering a need that bestows on them, whether dependent or independent, a sense of worth and of belonging.

"Honor thy father and thy mother: that thy days may be long upon the land which the Lord thy God giveth thee" (Exodus 20:12). Do we enough remember this Commandment, or has our commitment to it passed with our unfaith in the old gods? Are we too willing to hand over to another—to a social agency, a "fund," a hospital, "the Government"—responsibilities that properly are our own? We are society, and society cannot avoid or shun the problem of the aged; meeting it will require our best attitudes and understanding.

Old age should not mark merely the end of living; it should be instead the season to harvest the fruits of a full life, years of maturity and wisdom and of their rewards. Many elderly persons have special contributions to make to society; their opportunities should not be denied them. Unfortunately, too many men and women of good faculty are put out to pasture, like "well-run steeds," when their mature judgment and experience could be used to serve the common good.

"Teach us to number our days . . ." (Psalm 90:12) so that each of us will put away something enduring for our old age, complete a work undone, enjoy a useful hobby, serve the community, conserve material acquisitions for security. The self-respect and the dignity of the aged must be preserved. Tennyson aptly expressed in *Ulysses* what seems to be lacking in our times—a much needed reassessment of our attitude toward the aged, their aspirations, and the obligations of the family unit, of society at large and, not the least, of our government.

> Old age hath yet his honor and his toil;
> Death closes all; but something ere the end,
> Some work of noble note, may yet be done.

Jesus healing the sick.

152

26

Hewers of Flesh and
Drawers of Water

Honour a physician with the honour due him . . . for the Lord hath created
him.
For of the Most High cometh healing, and he shall receive honour of the
king.
The skill of the physician shall lift up his head: and in the sight of great men
he shall be in admiration.   Ecclesiasticus 38:1-3

Whence medicine? Whither? Have its specialties
helped or harmed its practice?

T HE ART OF HEALING is a natural craft conceived in sympathy
and born of necessity. The earliest medicine men were, as some
still may be, magicians, sorcerers, and witch doctors. Yet during
Egypt's zenith, three thousand years ago, medicine was so highly
organized that specialization had begun.

Herodotus the Greek historian, observed of the Egyptians: "The art
of medicine among them is distributed thus: each physician is a
physician of one disease and no more . . . and the whole country is full
of physicians." Some attended disorders of the eyes (ophthalmolo-
gists), others of the head (neurologists); some of the teeth (dentists),
others of the bowel (gastroenterologists); and still others attended
disorders perhaps less conspicuous and more general (diagnosticians).
Despite such "modernity," the Egyptian pharmacopoeia included,
along with good prescriptions, many that called for animal excreta,
lizard's blood, swine's teeth, putrid meat and stinking fat.

Moses, knowing the limitations of the medicine of his time, rejected
all of this, and formulated a concept of public hygiene to prevent
disease. Priests were appointed public health officers, the first sanitary
inspectors, and they put into effect the rules governing contagion:

isolation and disinfection. The Mosaic Code covered proper food, personal hygiene and communal health. Under it, medicinal preparations were concocted from spices and herbs, and soothing ointments from sheep fat and olive oil. Wounds were treated in the manner of the Good Samaritan, who "bound up his wounds, pouring in oil and wine" (Luke 10:34). The Hebrews' use of frankincense and myrrh, bark, aloes and cloves was superior to that of the Egyptians, many of whose bizarre formulas remained, however, a part of the apothecary's craft into the eighteenth century.

Moses, said de Musy, possessed "intuition prophetique des microbes." When most of the world considered disease a divine visitation or punishment, he recognized that some ills were communicable, that they could be controlled by forethought, and that contact could be reduced by isolation or quarantine.

Was it, one may wonder, a form of childbed fever that prompted Moses to consider an Israelitish woman unclean for seven days after childbearing and to exclude her from holy functions—with a group of others—for forty days? When the authorities of Venice and Marseilles suspected infection among the passengers of ships in the fourteenth century, they quarantined them for forty days. The Latin for forty is *quadraginta;* the Italian and French for forty days *quarantina* and *quarantaine*—our *quarantine,* of course. In A.D. 70, Titus brought to Rome from Jerusalem seventy thousand captives; they may well have introduced Moses' notion of forty days' isolation.

Moses practiced preventive medicine, Jesus psychosomatic. "And Jesus went about all Galilee, teaching in their synagogues, and preaching the gospel of the kingdom, and healing all manner of sickness and all manner of disease among the people" (Matthew 4:23), "people that were taken with divers diseases and torments, and those which were possessed with devils, and those which were lunatick, and those that had the palsy. . . ." Jesus knew that sickness is often the manifestation of a disturbed soul. To the man sick with palsy he said, not "Arise and walk," but, preferring to put his mind at ease, "Thy sins be forgiven thee" (Matthew 9:2).

Jesus' ministry was to the total human need. He knew what we have come to realize only recently: that much of our illness comes from broken interpersonal relations, from guilt and from the void where no love is. His earliest doctrine linked preaching with healing: "Heal the sick, cleanse the lepers, raise the dead, cast out devils" ((Matthew 10:8).

More than four centuries before Jesus, the system that became western medicine was developing under Hippocrates, "the Father of Medicine," in Greece. He set the pattern for professional attitudes and ethics, taught that observation and deduction were more important than textbook treatment, and emphasized the healing power of nature rather than of drugs. He and such giants as Aristotle, Celsus, and Dioscorides, in the following four centuries, influenced medicine for all time; but it was the great Greek physician, Galen (A.D. 131-200?), who modified and so perpetuated Hippocrates that he remained *the* authority for fourteen centuries, as often retarding as advancing medicine.

His father, he writes, "was amiable, just, and benevolent. My mother . . . had a very bad temper; she used to bite her serving maids, and was perpetually shouting at my father." Galen apparently inherited, writes Guthrie, the intelligence of his father, a successful architect, and the quarrelsome nature of his mother. He became physician to Emperor Marcus Aurelius Antoninus and, because of his four hundred works, the dictator of medicine.

And, as dictator, he laid a dead hand on medicine, despite his brilliance as observer and experimentalist. Much of his philosophy— nature acted, always, with perfect wisdom; the body was "the mere vehicle for the soul"—though friendly to the Church, was inimical to the growth of medicine as a science. As late as the seventeenth century, William Harvey, author of the *Anatomical Treatise on the Movement of the Heart and Blood in Animals,* possibly the greatest book in medical literature, was bitterly attacked by the Galenists of his time and university. Countless discoveries and regimens were rejected because they were not in Galen's works, the infallible source of knowledge.

Medicine entered the long period of bondage that we call the Middle Ages, a slave to conventions that discouraged learning, experiment and originality. The Church held that nothing could detract from the Great Physician and that disease was a punishment for sin; because the body was sacred, it forbade dissection. In A.D. 391, Christian fanatics burned the great library in Alexandria and destroyed priceless treasures of learning. Yet the Church also advanced medicine, with its pity for the ill and the monks' preservation of ancient medical works.

Chaucer said of his Doctor of Physic:

> Wel knew he the oldé Esculapius
> And Deiscorides, and eek Rufus
> Old Ypocras, Haly and Galien
> Serapion, Razis, and Avicen
> Averrios, Damascien, and Constantyn
> Bernard, and Gatesden, and Gilbertyn.

A second great preserver of medical knowledge during the Middle Ages was Arabian medicine, so called because of the language in which the physicians wrote. Few of them were Arabs: some were Syrian, some Persian, some Spanish, and many were Christians and Jews. They approved their predecessors, translated them into Arabic, wrote commentaries on the translations, and added observations of their own, especially on epidemic fevers and diseases of the eye, common in the East. They also made large contributions in pharmacology and its ally, alchemy or chemistry.

It fell to the lot of the Jewish physician to help safeguard the medical heritage. The twelfth-century Council of Rheims interdicted the study of law and of physic to monks, and later the Lateran Council forbade physicians, under pain of exclusion from the Church, to undertake medical treatment without ecclesiastical advice. So the plight of the Jewish physician in Europe of the Middle Ages was difficult. He was used and abused, a "sort of contraband luxury" resorted to by priest and prelate alike, yet hardly countenanced for any other reason. In an address on Morgagni in 1894, before the International Congress in Rome, the most famous of German pathologists, Virchow, said:

In our times Hebrew manuscripts have been brought to light which show with what zeal and learning Jewish physicians of early medieval times were active in the preservation and advancement of medicine.

The Renaissance dispelled much of the darkness of ten centuries, and gave to medical investigation a new lease on life. New and tragic diseases—syphilis, gunshot wounds—demanded attention; artists specialized in anatomy and dissection, chief amongst them Leonardo da Vinci; and Paracelsus (1493–1541) stimulated the revolt against dogmatism and roused men to seek new knowledge. He was perhaps the most original thinker of the sixteenth century: bold enough to discard Galenism, he presented the doctrine *similia similibus curantur* (like is cured by like), his "doctrine of signatures." The concept was that many diseases are cured by conditions (drugs) which produce a condition similar to the disease. In a measure, the doctrine was substantiated in 1796 when Edward Jenner, an English country doctor, introduced the practice of vaccination with cowpox for the prevention of smallpox. And in our own day, the use of typhoid and live "polio" virus vaccines, as well as the treatment of noncontagious disorders such as hay fever and allergies by minute but increasing doses of the offending pollen or allergen, is in consonance with the principle of *similia similibus curantur*.

The great medical leaders of the sixteenth century—Paracelsus, Paré, and Vesalius, the latter famed for the accuracy of his anatomical descriptions—blazed the way for the general advance of medicine to follow. Other notables of the era were the Spaniard, Michael Servetus, who first described the pulmonary circulation (1553), and the Englishman, William Harvey (1578-1657), who discovered the circulation of the blood and founded modern physiology.

Specialization was not completely resurrected until recent times, although given impetus by the Royal College of Physicians (formed under the guidance of a physician-priest, Thomas Linacre, in 1518), which regulated a physician's work and encouraged interest in particular fields of medicine. Notwithstanding the contributions of individual men throughout the Renaissance, witness the condition of medicine in England during the seventeenth century as recorded by Dr. Gideon Harvey. He classified the physicians into six sects: one, chalybeate doctors, who cured all diseases with preparations of steel or copper (much like the modern physicians who give iron and vitamins with minerals to all patients); two, medical ass-drivers, who put all their patients on diets of asses' milk (to this day, a diet of goat's milk is not infrequently prescribed); three, jesuitical doctors, who depended upon bark (quinine, originally obtained from Peruvian tree bark, is often used to differentiate malarial fever from other febrile illnesses); four, water bailiffs, who drenched their patients in the mineral springs (spas are still popular today); five, butcher doctors, who always bled their patients (some surgeons, afflicted with "furor operativa," still do); and six, illustrious muck doctors, who expelled diseases by

157

purgation (calomel is still used). Has the old order changed or do we now simply have a new set of categories: vitamin pill pushers, antibiotic enthusiasts, hormone hustlers, appendix apprehenders, mammary misogynists, dilation and curettage deceivers, uterine usurpers—hewers of flesh and drawers of water?

The physician of three hundred years ago was permitted to practice both medicine and surgery; his colleague, the surgeon—a man with certain mechanical or technical skills—was allowed only to perform surgery and not to presume to treat medical ailments. He was called not *Doctor* but *Mister*, which the surgeon in Great Britain, disdaining the generally more honored title, retains. Today, the order is reversed. The specialist in internal medicine may practice medicine but not surgery; the surgeon, on the other hand, performs surgery and often practices a great deal of medicine besides.

A bit of insight into the state of medical affairs in England early in the eighteenth century—when crab's-eye powder was still a medicament—may be gleaned from the quarrel between Bidloo, the Dutch doctor who was brought to England from the famed University of Leyden by King William III to serve as his personal physician, and Ronjat, the French surgeon who was also in the king's entourage. The king had fallen from his horse during the hunt, and his shoulder bone was believed to be broken. Bidloo wanted to put on the bandages but Ronjat objected vehemently, saying "C'est moi qui suis le premier chirurgien du Roi" (It is I who am the first surgeon to the King).

Though the Royal Society had spread the news of the amazing discoveries that were taking place, nevertheless there was much resistance to the progress that experimental methods had made possible. In such an atmosphere, there was no place for Harvey's *De Motu Cordis*, since Hippocrates, Galen and Avicenna had said nothing about circulation of the blood. As for Paracelsus, his name was blasphemy. In France, for instance, the Paris faculty zealously guarded their rights and privileges against all interlopers: apothecaries and barber-surgeons were classed as vile conspirators against the medical profession. Blood letting and purgation were the typical approach of the day; though Harvey and his successors had proved them nonsense, their use died slowly. Polypharmacy—prescriptions contained dozens of ingredients, including live worms, vipers' flesh, and bezoar stones—flourished. Guy Patin, spokesman of the Paris school at mid-seventeenth century, rightfully preached a return to simple remedies, and fought against the encroachments of new-fangled medicines, particularly the use of antimony. Incidentally, Patin also opposed the barber-surgeons since they, too, were trying to usurp the province of the academicians, but, thanks to a fistula in the royal anus (an ailment of Louis XIV), the surgeons soon moved up in status.

The petty jealousies that stigmatized French medicine gradually disappeared, and the nineteenth century ushered in a new era for France. Thanks to Napoleon's patronage, abundant facilities were provided for hospital care and, fortunately, the medical talent was ready: Paris became, for a time, the scientific capital of the world. The first stethoscope—today's symbol of the doctor—was invented by Réné-Théophile Laennec in 1816, and every physician who listens to the chest with this instrument will ever remain in his debt. The blessing of the nineteenth century was the uniting of science with medicine, a fact which Lord Lister of *asepsis* fame movingly pointed out in his memorable address on December 27, 1892, at the Sorbonne in Paris, when Louis Pasteur was honored by the world on the occasion of his seventieth birthday.

The modern "father of medicine," Sir William Osler—a product of the nineteenth century—said this of his times:

> To us in the medical profession . . . whose work is with the sick and suffering, the great boon of this wonderful century . . . is the fact that the leaves of the tree of Science have been for the healing of nations. This is the Promethean gift of the century to man.

It is the twentieth century, however, that has witnessed the greatest achievements in the biologic sciences. The technologic and scientific advances in medicine have been greater in the past fifty years than in all the years of our civilization. A prerequisite for our modern technical development is a very high degree of specialization: the necessity of subdividing knowledge as it expands has forced the creation of specialties and subspecialties.

Specialization in the medical arts proceeds at a fast pace today. Internal medicine is divided into a dozen or more specialites: allergy, dermatology, cardiology, gastroenterology, endocrinology and peripheral hematology. Surgery has gone just as far, with its abdominal, thoracic, gynecologic, urologic, vascular, plastic and neurologic surgeons, among others. No one will deny that all this indicates some sort of progress, but the boundary between one surgical specialty and another is frequently difficult to define. The urethra, the vagina and the rectum occupy so circumscribed an area that, literally, a fine line demarcates the province of the urologist, the gynecologist and the proctologist. One slip, and where is the surgeon?—in another's territory.

ˇThe human side of medicine has changed. Better educated and informed—often enough misinformed, also, by television, comic strips, and "feature articles"—the public knows more about diseases and their treatments, and the impact of science and social change has altered the patient's attitude toward his doctor. The patient has lost his awe, perhaps, of the physician, often divesting himself of the faith that also cures, especially in functional illness, and building within himself false images.

It would be folly to ignore the fact that the medical profession has lost face in our society. The image of the selfless, dedicated physician has been beclouded. But why? Is it that the "bedside manner" has disappeared because new diagnostic laboratory tests, specific drugs, technical equipment, and surgical skills have contributed to a change from a warm friendly relationship to one colder, more calculated, less personal—and that, although medical care is better by far than ever before, the medical profession has deteriorated in the public eye?

The mortality of acute pneumonia has been reduced from twenty-five per cent and more to one per cent and, frequently, all that is required of the patient is to swallow eight pills a day. In a former day, the physician labored for days, keeping a fearful vigil with the family as the patient approached a successful crisis, or his demise. The family physician then had few tools, but he offered warmth, comfort and his unhurried attentions; today he has too often appeared to be a cold, calculating instrument of science. The emotional disenchantment between patient and physician started with the vanishing family doctor and the emergence of the specialist. Depth of personal understanding has yielded to breadth of medical knowledge.

Perhaps the objective methodology inherited from Hippocratic medicine of yesteryear and the impersonal precision and efficiency of present-day specialists are not enough. Sympathy and love identified with the healing acts of Jesus, and the concern for the healthy individual as the unit of communal welfare, as bequeathed to us by Moses, are ingredients that are missing in the prescriptions for the ills of mankind.

As the panorama of the healing art unfolds, one cannot fail to be impressed by the changing image of the healer. The need for the physician ever increases, for the sick will always be with us. In spite of the progress made in the last century, the physically ill and the mentally distraught fill our hospitals to overflowing, and one is constrained to ask with Jeremiah:

> Is there no balm in Gilead; is there no physician there? why then is not the health of the daughter of my people recovered?   Jeremiah 8:22

The Oath of Hippocrates has traditionally served as the standard of ethical practice, but no more beautiful guide may be found than the lesser known *Oath and Prayer of Moses Maimonides,* twelfth-century physician. This reads, in part:

> O, grant—
> That neither greed for gain, nor thirst for fame,
>   nor vain ambition,
> May interfere with my activity.
> For these I know are enemies of truth and love
>   of men,
> And might beguile one in my profession
> From furthering the welfare of Thy creatures.
> O strengthen me.
> Grant energy unto both body and the soul
> That I might e'er unhindered ready be
> To mitigate the woes,
> Sustain and help
> The rich and poor, the good and bad, enemy
>   and friend.
> O let me e'er behold in the afflicted and suffering,
> Only the human being.

Delilah cuts off Samson's hair and deprives him of strength.

27

In Faint Praise of Hair

Doth not even nature itself teach you, that, if a man have long hair, it is a
shame unto him?
But if a woman have long hair, it is a glory to her
1 Corinthians 11:14-15

*Why has long hair held a strange fascination for
some men?*

IN ALL GENERATIONS, the male with a luxuriant head of hair
has been an object of admiration or derision, depending on the
time, the clime and the mood of the people; whereas the bald-headed
man has ever been the butt of humor and ridicule. Recall that in
biblical days, the children mocked the prophet Elisha, shouting "Go
up, thou bald head; go up, thou bald head" (2 Kings 2:23). Shakespeare,
however, tried to temper our demeanor toward the bald-headed man,
for he wrote in his *Comedy of Errors,* "What he hath scanted men in
hair, he hath given them in wit."

One cannot help but wonder about today's trend. Not so many years
ago, it was only women who frequented beauty parlors for hair
styling, permanents, sprays, coloring and conditioners. Today's "unisex" salon caters to both sexes. Many men now demand the touch of a
fashionable stylist to groom their hair. Does this imply, as some
psychologists say, that we are indeed embarking on a unisex era? Or
is it simply another chapter in man's preoccupation with his hair?

The mystique associated with the fullness and length of head hair is
not novel. The story of Samson equated long hair with power. Samson,
you will remember, became enamored with the glamorous Delilah. In
the pay of Philistine overlords, she was to learn the source of the
superhuman strength of the man who slew five hundred Philistines
with the jawbone of an ass. One day, he revealed the secret to his
paramour with these words: "There hath not come a razor upon mine

head; for I have been a Nazarite unto God from my mother's womb: if I be shaven, then my strength will go from me" (Judges 16:17). The Nazarite, under ancient Hebrew law, took an oath to abstain from wine, to wear long and uncut hair, and to refrain from contact with the dead.

While Samson was overcome with the sweet exhaustion that follows a night filled with love, the treacherous Delilah gave him the most infamous haircut in all history. Samson was reduced to a weak and helpless shadow of a man, imprisoned and blinded by his enemies. The loss of his hair proved his undoing. Ah, but when his hair grew again, Samson tasted revenge, however briefly, when he brought down the temple on his tormentors!

This is probably not the whole story. The mental anguish Samson must have suffered on learning that he, a Nazarite, had been shorn of his hair was great enough to throw him into a physical decline. His fate paralleled that of an older legendary tribal hero who lost his strength when his "woman" emasculated him during a deep sleep. Thus weakened, he fell into the hands of the enemy.

For yet another biblical personality, the retention of his hirsute adornment proved equally catastrophic. Absalom, the vain and conceited son of King David, was renowned for his "beauty" and the abundance of his head hair. He led his sycophants in an uprising against the King. When the battle was lost, and while in headlong retreat astride his mule, his hair became entangled in the thick boughs of an oak tree. There, he hung suspended "between the heaven and the earth" (2 Samuel 18:9) and was easy prey for Joab, one of David's captains. Absalom was slain. His hair, though a source of great pride, ultimately proved his nemesis.

Throughout the centuries, long and luxuriant head hair has had some strange fascination for man. In his phylogenetic development, man emerged not only erect but void of much of the thick pelage which covers the bodies of all primates. But of all human and subhuman forms, only man has the capacity to grow excessively long head hair. Although head hair, as opposed to beard growth, axillary and pubic hair, is not primarily hormonally dependent, it is considerably modified by hormones. It is safe to say that baldness in men follows a genetic pattern, tempered by the individual hormonal milieu.

Degrees of baldness are also seen in women without obvious endocrinopathies, though mild to marked recession of the hairline of the forehead is usually a feature in a woman virilized by an endocrine disorder or tumor. Queen Elizabeth I lost most of her hair during her bout with smallpox, resorting thereafter, to the use of a wig of brilliant red hair. Males castrated in their youth may not become bald, despite a familial history of baldness; and bald men have been known, on occasion, to regrow head hair following castration, a rather drastic solution to prevent falling hair. Nevertheless, the eunuch has enjoyed a gentle place in history. In Chaucer's *Canterbury Tales*, the gentle Pardoner has come straight from the court of Rome, "The Pardoner had hair as yellow as wax . . . his locks hung down . . . over his shoulders . . ." The Pardoner was quite effeminate, had a high-pitched voice, and "no beard did he have, nor would ever have." He was evidently eunuchoid.

The balding Louis XIII hit on a simpler and quite fashionable solution—the decorative wig. Later, when England's Charles II was exiled to France, these wigs struck his fancy and he brought back the fashion to his homeland in 1660, when he was restored to the throne. His courtiers followed his example. As the vogue spread through Europe, it became the style of the affluent. Wig wearing, naturally connected with nobility, became a symbol of honor and culture. When the pressure of national problems caused Englishmen to forsake this expensive fashion, the Lord Chancellor, the judges, and the barristers decided to retain the custom. The wig is still worn in the courts of England and serves as a reminder that justice and integrity of the law are continual and unchanging—at least in theory.

Sociologists and psychologists have had a field day with the more current symbolism attached to hair, especially the long-haired male spawned by the Beatles in the 1960's. Of course, history is full of long-haired rebels and original thinkers.

Jesus is pictured in most art with long, flowing hair and a full beard. Although he did not proclaim himself to be a revolutionary, his words and deeds conveyed that he was a "rebel" in the best sense of the word. Flavius Josephus, the great Jewish historian of the first century who chronicled the wars of the Jews and Romans, is portrayed with long hair, as was Mohammed (seventh century), Moses Maimonides (twelfth century), Martin Luther (sixteenth century), Victor Hugo (eighteenth century), Walt Whitman (nineteenth century), and Albert Einstein and George Bernard Shaw (twentieth century). Poets and painters, statesmen and politicians often distinguished themselves by their hair styles—from George Washington to John Kennedy, Disraeli to Lloyd George, Mozart to Stravinsky, Milton to Ernest Hemingway, to mention just a few. During the War between the States, many of the generals on both sides had flowing locks, signifying position and intimating gallantry.

In the 1960's, long hair became the hallmark of the beatnick, the hippie, the disenchanted, the individualist. Hair length and style reflected the mood of the day. For several years, it symbolized sexual freedom, dissent, defiance, dissatisfaction with the status quo. For many, it became a badge, proclaiming abhorrence of the Vietnam war. For this latter group, it carried an unmistakable message—that peace is not absence of war, but the presence of justice—and they sought to right the wrongs, real and imagined. Too often, there are groups who protest, not knowing for what or why, merely for the sake of protesting. Many a hippie is genuinely concerned with the fate of the world about him. He is willing to do away with worldly goods, to forswear materialistic things, and is content to return to nature. He shares the alarm of Oliver Goldsmith, who in the *Deserted Village,* warned, "Ill fares the land, to hastening ills a prey, where wealth accumulates, and men decay." For the sensitive, hirsute appendages express the haunting desire, experienced by each individual, to lose his sense of isolation and to identify with other humans who share their inner discontent. It is their "thing." The right to their plumage is theirs. It cannot be legislated.

But at times the symbols became confused. Some of our most fervent antiwar protests were directed against the late President Lyndon B. Johnson, with the long-hairs lined up on the side of peace and the short-hairs on the side of war. It was also young against old, sexually liberated versus the conventional. But the images can change as quickly as hair grows, and before his death, Lyndon Johnson sported an over-the-collar mane of silver hair. Even pictures of former President Nixon's arch aide, H. R. Haldeman, showed that he had let his hair grow long. However, in the mid-70's a resurgence of short-hair styles as the "in" thing gained momentum.

Somewhat amusing is the fact that the Apostle Paul, in his first letter to the Corinthians, took a dim view of the long-haired of his time. Perhaps, if viewed through the eyes of some demagogue, one may interpret youth's uninhibited hair growth as some sort of Communist conspiracy—a revolt against the fundamental teaching of Christianity and encouragement against established order.

There is nothing new in the periodic craze for long hair, except that in the latter part of the twentieth century it was not so much a manifestation of a wolf in sheep's clothing, as it was, perhaps, a sheep in wolf's clothing.

What does all this prove? It certainly shows that there is nothing new in the obsession with hair, and further it proves that one cannot judge a man's worth by the length of his hair. But if history has any lesson for the present, we may rest assured that whatever the fad, chic, or symbol is at any particular time, it too will undoubtedly pass. The pendulum undoubtedly will swing in the opposite direction.

Bonnat's vivid picture of Job's suffering.

168

28

Job's Dilemma

His breasts are full of milk, and his bones are moistened with marrow.
                                                                    Job 21:24

> *Can men and virgin women lactate, or are such
> reports purely mythical?*

A MOTHER NURSING HER INFANT provokes no mystery, but lactation unrelated to pregnancy presents a curious phenomenon. Milk secretion in the male, however, begs for credence. The idea of a spontaneous flow of milk (galactorrhea) in the male seems so incredible that its mention in the Bible was regarded as erroneous. Many biblical scholars, confused by the passage, "His breasts are full of milk" (Job 21:24), apologetically offered another interpretation, such as "His vessels [pails] are full of milk" (late Hebrew version); "His pectorals are fat-laden" (Greek); "His viscera are full of fat" (Latin), "His flanks are full of fat" (French). Actually there is no need for an exegesis of the version found in the Geneva Bible of 1594, "His breasts are full of milke, and his bones run full of marowe" or in the King James Version of the Holy Bible. Scholars in preparing the Revised Standard Version (RSV) have retrenched from the original position and subverted Job 21:24 to "his body full of fat." This is indeed unfortunate because the recently published Targum (Aramaic translation) recovered from Cave XI of Khirbet Qumran in the Judean wilderness speaks of "His teats are full of milk."*

Mythology has perpetuated legends of men with breasts resembling those of women, not only in size but also in function. Chinese legendary literature relates that Pi-Kou, after the death of his foster parents, kept their two little daughters alive by having them suckle at his own breast. Actual cases are also on record. The Bishop of Cork

*Job by Marvin H. Pope, Doubleday & Co., N.Y., 1965.

(1738) witnessed an elderly man nursing his own child. A twenty-two year-old soldier, from whose swollen breasts two ounces of milk could be expressed in twenty-four hours, was the subject of a medical report in 1837; and the Berlin Anthropological Society was informed in 1864 that a gigantic man nursed his son from one of his strongly developed breasts. The Talmud records the case of a man who, when his wife died leaving him a young infant, could not afford a wet nurse. Then, *mirabile dictu*, his breasts expanded like the two breasts of a woman, and he suckled his son.

Enlargement of the breasts (gynecomastia) was observed following the refeeding of malnourished prisoners of World War II. Because these changes occurred while the men were recovering from malnutrition and not during the period of inanition, the phenomenon was called the inanition-refeeding syndrome. Furthermore, the appearance of milky or colostrumlike secretions was not an isolated happening. In a study of three hundred cases of gynecomastia in former war prisoners, Jacobs found that nine had milky secretions from their breasts. It is not farfetched to assume that the author of Job was dealing with a similar situation. It will be recalled that Job, in his affliction, could not eat and was wasting away, "My bone cleaveth to my skin and to my flesh, and I am escaped with the skin of my teeth" (Job 19:20). Later, the Bible tells us that, "His flesh is consumed away . . . his bones . . . stick out" (33:21). After Job proved his steadfastness in his beliefs and his dedication to the Lord, he regained his health as further challenges to his faith were removed. Then the author of Job could truthfully write that, "His bones are moistened with marrow [recovery to health], and his breasts are full of milk [gynecomastia with galactorrhea]." More than two millennia elapsed before some scientific basis could be offered for the mystique of inappropriate lactation in man.

The phenomenon of lactation and loss of menses (amenorrhea) in virginal women, or in those who have never been pregnant, has been known for over two-thousand years. Hippocrates observed that "If a woman is not with child, nor has brought forth, have milk, her menses are obstructed." Moses Maimonides, twelfth-century physician, in his book on aphorisms, also called attention to this condition.

Galactorrhea has always seemed more legendary than credible in men harboring pituitary gland tumors resulting in gigantism or gross enlargement of their cartilaginous and soft tissue, giving them a bulldog appearance—acromegaly. Its presence in acromegalic women has been accepted as commonplace. Pituitary tumor in association with amenorrhea-lactation, but unrelated to giantism or acromegaly, is no longer considered a rare occurrence and more and more cases are being reported in the medical annals. Furthermore, aside from persistent amenorrhea and galactorrhea after normal parturition (Chiari-Frommel syndrome), many cases of amenorrhea and galactorrhea are being encountered in women following discontinuation of the birth-control pill. This unusual physiologic disorder of abnormal lactation with or without loss of menstruation also has been observed in women ingesting large doses of certain psychotropic drugs. In a recent study of two hundred females with galactorrhea following the use of tranquilizing agents, this complication appeared about twice as often (76%) in women who had lactated previously following pregnancy. In the same study, galactorrhea appeared in six of sixty males treated with psychotropic drugs.

Abnormal milk secretion in both males and females should not take one by surprise any longer. Folklore is rich in fables depicting lactation in nonpregnant women, grandmothers and fathers. Livingstone, the great explorer of Africa, saw several instances among the Bechuana tribes in which the grandmother had undertaken to suckle her grandchild. Lafitau, a missionary to American Indians, relates that among the Iroquois, should a baby lose its mother, the grandmother knew how to make her breasts produce milk. The Berliner Wochenblatt (1812), under the superscription "Naturwunder: Die saugenda Grossmutter," described the case of Marguerite Francesca Laloitette, wife of a Parisian water carrier, who at seventy-one years of age nursed her grandchild. For two months prior to the birth of the child, she prepared for the event by having her breasts suckled by children and young dogs. The granddaughter enjoyed good health and teethed at the proper time. In rural Georgia, grandmothers have been known to place puppy dogs to their breasts in preparation for the task of becoming the wet nurse for the offspring of an expectant, but sickly daughter.

From the beginning of recorded history, grandmothers have been wet nurses. The Bible related that when Ruth married Boaz and bore a child, the neighbors came twittering around Naomi, her mother-in-law, proclaiming,". . . and he shall be . . . a nourisher of thine old age . . . and Naomi took the child, and laid it in her bosom and became nurse unto it" (Ruth 4:15-16).

Some years ago, there appeared in the nationally syndicated "Dear Abby" column a request for advice. A young, unmarried woman was about to adopt a newborn infant and wanted to know if, by taking hormones, it would be possible for her to nurse the child. Abby, after conferring with her medical consultants, replied that the scheme was preposterous and gratuitously pointed out that hormones would only grow unwanted hair. Several indignant readers wrote to say that they had known of instances in which such women nursed infants successfully by persistently placing the child to the breast. Moreover, a young mother claimed that her younger sister had begun to lactate spontaneously in a seemingly sympathetic response to certain difficulties that the young mother was experiencing.

Lactation in normally parturient women is sometimes purposely prolonged for two or three years in the belief that conception will not occur while a woman is actively nursing a child—a belief that is rather widespread among the more primitive peoples of the world. However, tribal experience has taught some that lactation is not always protective against conception and the taboo against sexual relations while lactating is in vogue in many parts of Africa and the islands of the South Pacific. For instance, the Yoruba women of West Africa breast-feed for eighteen months while practicing abstinence—the only sure method of preventing conception. This taboo may have as its basis the importance of conserving the milk supply for the breast-fed infant, or the need to prevent the added burden of another pregnancy to the already overburdened mother. Our wise ancestral fathers appreciated the fact that lactation is not a sure method of conception control, because they permitted coitus interruptus to be practiced in this circumstance. Although onanism (coitus interruptus) was condemned by the ancient Hebrews, Rabbi Eleazor, First Century A.D., condoned this contraceptive procedure during lactation. He stated that a man may "thresh inside but winnow outside," in order that a husband not be denied while the woman continued to be protected, or so it was hoped.

The fascinating phenomenon of lactation has intrigued man from the beginning of time. The nursing mother provides sustenance for the suckling infant, but only so long as stimulation by suckling is continued. The suckling reflex plays a major role not only in maintenance of the supply of milk but also in initiating lactation in women who have never been pregnant, as well as in men, by persistently stimulating the breast through suckling. The sixteenth century Venetian master, Tintoretto, in his painting "The Origin of the Milky Way," vividly illustrates the forceful ejection of a stream of milk from the contra-lateral breast as Jupiter plucks the suckling infant, Hercules, from Juno's breast.

With recent advances in our knowledge of lactation, it has been determined that psychophysical disturbances and disorders of the endocrine glandular system are responsible for such curiosities as lactation in males and in virgin females. The mystique surrounding inappropriate galactorrhea in man and woman is no longer the perplexing enigma of by-gone years. We can confidently say that the translation in Job, "His breasts are full of milk," was not simply a figure of speech.

The Day of Judgement – William Blake's illustration "The Grave".

29

Sexual Apostasy

And if thy right eye offend thee, pluck it out, and cast it from thee;
For it is profitable for thee that one of thy members should perish, and not
that thy whole body should be cast into hell.   Matthew 5:29

How should society regard voluntary emasculation?

MODERN SOCIETY is toying with a new sense or code of sexual
values. The lusty sensuality of the Old Testament was basic and
earthy. Recall how the Song of Solomon proclaimed with more charm
than innocence "he shall lie all night betwixt my breasts" (Song of
Solomon 1:13), or the poet of the Proverbs who admonished, "Let her
breasts satisfy thee at all times; and be thou ravished always with her
love" (Proverbs 5:18-19). With the advent of Christianity, a change in
attitude took place and the Church combined the Jewish ennoblement
of sex for procreation (be fruitful and multiply) with the sacred state
of chastity (the Greco-Indian ideal of sexual abstinence), placing the
greatest possible restriction on sexual feeling—a sort of joyless
sexuality. Witness the advice of the Apostle Paul to those who would
serve God with the same singlemindedness as he did: "They that have
wives be as though they had none" (1 Corinthians 7:29); or "It is good
for a man not to touch a woman . . . but if they cannot contain, let
them marry: for it is better to marry than to burn" (1 Corinthians 7:1,
9). The basic rift between spirit and nature which has so troubled the
Western world may be traced back to such early Pauline teachings. If
there is a sexual revolution that is destroying cherished traditions and
taboos, if there is greater permissiveness, a new morality, and a
"deterioration" in our mores, then it may be construed as a revolt
against an insufferable ethic that sex has to be related to love or
procreation alone. Paul's attitudes on sexual morality have increas-
ingly been contested by more liberal theologians. For instance, all but

completely suppressed at Catholic nuptial liturgies of late is the traditional reading from Paul's epistle to the Ephesians: "Wives, submit yourselves unto your own husbands, as unto the Lord. For the husband is the head of the wife . . ." (5:22-23).

The Judeo-Christian views on sexual behavior are being ignored. Permissiveness, promiscuity, mate swapping, menage à trois, and voluptuous sex orgies now extant throughout the land, equal those that plagued ancient Rome. Homosexuality is now regarded as a mere aberration, lesbianism is countenanced, tranvestism abounds, and the desire for sexual reorientation is no longer an isolated phenomenon.

Christine Jorgensen, the transsexual who gained worldwide notoriety twenty years ago, addressed a group of students at the University of Minnesota. While discussing the women's liberation movement, "she" stated that men need to be liberated too. Recalling her operation, she added, "I can look back and see that this was the beginning of a sexual revoltuion." But did Christine Jorgensen really start a sexual revolution? Was her sexual transformation something new? *Nihil novi.* Historians record that the Roman Emperor Nero, in a public ceremony, married the eunuch Sporus who was attired in feminine dress. Sporus, a spadone (only testes were removed) underwent, so it was rumored, another operation in order to become as much like a female as possible.

Eunuchs were popular in decadent Rome. They became the playmates, the objects of sexual orgies of many well-known Romans of the day; Octavius, Tiberius, and Caligula made spectacles of themselves. Eunuchs became the darlings of the wealthy and were much sought after by the great ladies of Rome, particularly if they were castrated after maturity. Such spadones do not necessarily lose their sexual potential. Many of the eunuchs of this particular era were voluntary emasculates because they enjoyed their role in society and because they felt more feminine than masculine.

Early in the history of mankind, castration was performed by the Egyptians, Persians, Assyrians and others as a means of subjugating their vanquished enemies. The function of castration was to keep human beings in a state of submissiveness, just as the gelding of stallions or castration of bulls makes them willing beasts of burden. The forceful castration of humans once was big business. Castrates, being quite docile, were sold for high prices on the slave market because they proved to be faithful servants and harem guards. Thus, the operation, usually removal of testes only, but at times of the total genitals, was performed to subjugate man and to tame him.

In the court of Nebuchadnezzar, king of Babylon, there evidently were a number of eunuchs serving. It was the "prince of the eunuchs" who looked on Daniel with "favour and tender love." He interceded with the king for Daniel and his friends to absolve these Israelites from obedience to the command to eat "the king's meat" and wine, food which was forbidden them by Hebrew law.

The cult of the eunuch reached its zenith in China where eunuchs held considerable power for two-thousand years. Until A.D. 618, most of China's eunuchs were obtained from conquered tribes, but during the T'ang Dynasty the need was greater than the supply, and the castration of volunteers was encouraged. More and more males of lowly birth sought this opportunity, since it would admit them to the palace where they would be given the level of work to which they were best suited. It became the custom for eunuchs to give sex education in early childhood to future emperors; others were chosen to instruct imperial princes in deportment, speech, etiquette and knowledge. Eunuchs grew in power because most of the ministers-of-state and indispensables were chosen from their lot. Chinese eunuchs influenced twenty-five dynasties and their services were not abolished until November 5, 1924, when the last emperor of the Ch'ing Dynasty was overthrown.

In many civilizations there are records of men who, by choice, behaved like women. Thirty centuries ago, this aberration was linked with religious customs in the worship of certain Babylonian deities. In another part of the world, the Aztecs encouraged emasculation for the sole reward of being a religious consecrate. In the remote past, eunuchs became so for religious reasons. They firmly believed that a state of sinlessness could be attained only by cutting off the offending organ. Castration was an ancient religious rite, but it was taken seriously by numerous early Christians. They based their belief on the words of Jesus, "And if thy right eye offend thee, pluck it out, and cast it from thee; for it is profitable for thee that one of thy members should perish, and not that thy whole body should be cast into hell," (Matthew 5:29), equating these words with "and there be eunuchs, which have made themselves eunuchs for the kingdom of heaven's sake" (19:12). Accordingly, the most celebrated voluntary castrate in all Christendom was Origen (A.D. 185–254). The *Encyclopaedia Britannica* describes him as the most distinguished and most influential of all theologians with the possible exception of Augustine. Origen castrated himself so that he might work unhindered in the instruction of women.

Eunuchs held considerable political power not only in China but also in Turkey. In Byzantium, during the reign of Constantine II, eunuchs were given precedence over the uncastrated male in the civil service, and many young patricians underwent voluntary emasculation in order to obtain important posts. Many rose to high rank in the Army and Navy. One of the most famous was Narses, the General who drove the Goths from Italy. In 1453, when the Byzantium Empire and its institutions fell before the Ottoman Turks, the palace eunuchs were retained in office. Such palace eunuchs held key positions into the early part of the twentieth century. The Turks had continued the system that enabled the sultan, by sexual repression, to maintain absolute control through an hierarchy of castrated males. (See chap. 8.)

The transformation of hermaphrodites and pseudohermaphrodites into the sex consonant with their psychic and emotional drives has been performed quite frequently and in most instances with a modicum of success. Quite dubious, however, are the end results of surgery that transforms a male into a female, or a female into a male, although the operation is being performed with increasing frequency in the United States and abroad. Dr. Walter Alvarez wrote with great sympathy on the subject and detailed the wrong that was righted in his patient, Miss Hedy Jo Star (formerly Mr. Carl Hammonds). Though Hollywood, by producing Gore Vidal's novel, *Myra Breckenridge,* has glamorized the transsexual, can it be said that "All's well that ends well"? Witness the fate of a moderately successful author who married "her" chauffeur, following sex transformation. Some months after the marriage, this newly constituted female began to experience pseudocyesis (i.e., false signs of pregnancy). "Her" emotional instability evidently had not been resolved by the operative procedure. *Mens sana in corpore sano!*

On the other hand, sexual change seemingly brought contentment to the troubled soul of James Morris, now Jan Morris. James was no effete dandy, but a highly successful journalist, author and world traveler, who was rugged enough to climb twenty-thousand feet of Mount Everest with Sir Edmund Hillary's party in 1953. From early childhood, James believed that he was indeed a female in a male body.

All his adult life he was tormented by the gnawing belief that his gender, his inner self, his very soul, was feminine. He felt that sooner or later he must satisfy an agonizing need for unity between sex and gender or destroy himself. In his book, *Conundrum*, the compelling forces that haunted him until he became Jan are revealed. The question arises: What distinguishes the homosexual, the transvestite, the bisexual, from the transsexual?

Was James Morris a homosexual? At school, as a rather attractive boy, it did not seem inappropriate to play a girl's role. He enjoyed being kissed and was distinctly flattered when the best looking boy in the dormitory made advances. He indulged in illicit pleasures and recalled the "clumsy embraces of one Bolsover Major" and "his sinuous techniques of trouser removal." One might look upon these experiences as boyhood whims during a phase when his sexual identity had not jelled. Later, as a subaltern in the famous 9th Queen's Royal Lancers he realized that he was fundamentally different from his male contemporaries. Although he much enjoyed the company of girls, he had no desire to sleep with them. His libidinous fancies were concerned more with caress than copulation. He mused that he was really pining for a man's love—yet, he states that he "certainly did not feel himself to be a homosexual."

Was he a transvestite? Some female impersonators frequently are latent or overt homosexuals; others are not, but delight in wearing the garb of the opposite sex. Morris envied women their clothes only as the outward sign of their femininity. However, after he started on estrogens in preparation for his ultimate crossover, he also assumed the unisex form of dress (i.e., jeans and sweater) so that people often asked, "Are you a man or a woman?"

Was he a bisexual? Throughout his young manhood, he was in a constant state of emotional entanglement—sometimes men, sometimes women. He finally met a woman with whom he had great rapport—married her and fathered five children, and in complete fidelity lived with her for some twenty years. But each year his longing to live as a woman grew more urgent and finally he could not stand his falsity any longer; he took the steps that irretrievably altered his body to fit his conviction—to match sex to gender; not half man and half woman, but a completely unified individual.

Transsexualism is a passionate, lifelong, ineradicable longing—that goes far beyond sex—to escape from maleness into womanhood or vice versa. Transsexuals often are psychotic exhibitionists or misguided homosexuals in search of legality, and only a few find happiness and fulfillment in their sexual reorientation. (See Chap. 17.)

From the endocrinologists point of view, I have always regarded sexual behavior as the expression of multiple complexities, such as chromosomal endowment, gender identification, gonadal adequacy, hormonal factors, childhood rearing, environmental influences, and possibly conditioning of the higher brain centers (the hypothalamus) during fetal life by maternal steroid hormones.

Of the Christine Jorgensen syndrome, the voluntary emasculate, let it be said that transsexuals are not necessarily homosexuals or lesbians. The general public, however, looks upon such transformations as a form of sexual apostasy. The former Vice President, Spiro Agnew, in trying to purge Senator Charles Goodell of New York, called him the "Christine Jorgensen" of the Republican Party. Thus, usage of this opprobrium has become a symbol of apostasy, whether political or sexual.

The idea of sexual overlap has always fascinated poets and myth makers. Early in Genesis the Bible states that God created man in his own image: "Male and female created he them" (1:27). Myths and history alike depict men who lived as women; women who lived as men; and men who, by self-mutilation, voluntarily changed to female roles. A little more than twenty years have elapsed since Christine Jorgensen gave inpetus to a movement that has reached endemic proportions—the compulsion for sex reorientation. For several years, a team at Johns Hopkins Hospital has been performing sex reassignment surgery on two patients per month; the waiting list is long. Several centers in this country and abroad offer this service. Voluntary emasculates are to be found in most countries of the world. Recently, several segments of a popular television series were devoted to the story of the sex change of a surgeon, eliciting at least awareness of the emotional torture of such a person, if not sympathy for him.

Throughout the centuries, males have subjugated themselves to castration or become eunuchs by their own hand either for religious reasons, or in the hope of gaining security and even material success. History records that eunuchs, both voluntary and involuntary, played diverse roles, from cooks and chamberlains to generals, from transvestite wives of Roman Emperors to fathers of the Church. Now we are confronted by a different type of would-be eunuch who opts for sexual transformation. Such persons claim that they are female personages imprisoned in male bodies and wish to be liberated from their masculine bonds by surgery and hormone therapy. Christine Jorgensen, the voluntary emasculate, the sexual apostate, started a trend by which feminine-oriented males could unloose the shackles that bind them to convention and become free to seek a newer world, to satisfy some inner drive, an inexplicable soul-hunger.

"... Yet I planted thee a noble vine, wholly a right seed; how then are thou turned into the degenerate plant of a strange vine ..." Jeremiah 2:21 (Vitis Orientalis).

30

Strange Bedfellows

If a man also lie with mankind, as he lieth with a woman, both of them have committed an abomination.   Leviticus 20:13

Is homosexuality on the rise, or has the moral climate made it possible to be open about it?

HOMOSEXUALITY, THE MOST COMMON form of sexual deviation, has existed from earliest times. Some societies, such as the ancient Greeks, tolerated it; others condemned it. The Hebrews of biblical days and the Christians from the time of the Apostle Paul have regarded homosexuality as a sin and a crime. Greece, with its exaltation of deviant love, represents one end of the spectrum; Israel's stern prohibition and violent punishment stands at the other.

The earliest encounter with homosexuality in the Old Testament tells of the two angels who came to the wicked city of Sodom to warn Lot that God was bent on destroying the city. Abraham pleaded that it be spared because of the good people dwelling therein, but when he could not produce even ten righteous men, the city was doomed. The two angels were guests in Lot's house when the men of Sodom surrounded it and called out to Lot, "Bring them out unto us, that we may know them." Lot refused, but offered instead his two daughters, who had not "known" man, to do unto them whatever they pleased. The next day, Lot, his wife and two daughters departed, and the twin cities of Sodom and Gomorrah were destroyed. To this day, men who seek to "know" others of their own sex are called sodomites.

Israel's pagan neighbors in the Fertile Crescent used male cult prostitutes in their exaltation of sexuality as the creative principle in nature. Sacred homosexuality, borrowed from the Canaanite cults, also was being practiced in Judah when Aza "put away the male cult prostitutes out of the land." At a later date, King Josiah broke down the houses of cult prostitutes that adjoined the temples. In Leviticus the

Hebrews were clearly admonished, "If a man lies with a male as with a woman, both of them have committed an abomination; they shall be put to death, their blood is upon them" (20:13 R.S.V.)

Julius Caesar, it is said, gave his virginity to King Nicomedes, and was therafter known as the Queen of Bithynia. Caesar debauched not only the wives but the sons and daughters of his friends and enemies. Curio said of him that he was "every woman's man, and every man's woman."

The warmth and affection which adolescent boys or girls display toward others of their own sex need not imply physical love but merely what has come to be known as "brotherly love." The Bible tells of David, the young musician, brought to the royal court to assuage King Saul's melancholy and ease his anguish. While in the palace he was befriended by the King's son, Jonathan. A true and abiding friendship developed, deep, intense and genuine, and "Saul's son delighted much in David" (1 Samuel 19:1). The relationship exemplified a love greater and more ennobling than that between man and woman, for it was brotherly love in its highest sense, "The soul of Jonathan was knit with the soul of David, and Jonathan loved him as his own soul" (1 Samuel 18:1).

The attraction between the two has been seized upon by some as an example of homosexual love. On learning that Jonathan perished in battle, David lamented, "I am distressed for thee, my brother Jonathan: very pleasant hast thou been unto me: thy love to me was wonderful, passing the love of women" (2 Samuel 1:26). For many scholars, the high praise accorded the love between these two youths was reminiscent of the spirit that pervades Plato's *Symposium*. The Greeks found beauty magnetic without respect to sex, and many amongst them believed that there was no higher form of love than homosexual love. However, the insinuation that the tender companionship of David and Jonathan was anything other than spiritual is without foundation. The whole affair reminds one of the accusation that William Shakespeare was homosexual because of some lines found in his sonnets which exalt a man's love for another man. By such lines as, "But since she prick't thee out for women's pleasure Mine be thy love, and thy love's use their treasure" (Sonnet 20), or "Two loves I have . . . the better angel is a man right fair" (Sonnet 144), he was merely showing his heartfelt appreciation to his patron. Nonetheless, Oscar Wilde, trenchant homosexual, used these lines and others to impugn the Bard of Avon. Homosexuals have done their utmost to annex Shakespeare and to use him as an advertisement of their own peculiarity. So too, has the ennobling friendship of David and Jonathan been misinterpreted. David was a sentimental man who loved greatly and felt deeply. When his own son, Absalom, was killed in armed rebellion against him, this sentimentality came to the fore. In his grief, David wailed, "Would God I had died for thee, O Absalom, my son, my son." (2 Samuel 18:33).

The Apostle Paul, who traveled widely, became aware of the widespread problem prevalent in the Greco-Roman world. In his Epistle to the Romans, he warns of the wrath of God upon those who dishonor their bodies, "And likewise also the men, leaving the natural use of the woman, burned in their lust one toward another; men with men working that which is unseemly, and receiving in themselves that recompence of their error which was meet" (Romans 1:27).

The attitudes expressed in the Old and the New Testaments have entered deeply into the texture of Western civilization. However, in recent years, in many countries and in several states of the Union, a more tolerant look at the problem is emerging. The laws against sexual deviation have recently been modified in cases of consenting adults.

Liberalized legislation and a more charitable attitude toward him has allowed the homosexual to come out into the open, indeed to demand certain rights. Organized groups of "gay" persons are boldly and actively campaigning for equal job opportunities, nondiscriminatory housing, federal and state legislation permitting them to marry. They are aggressively seeking to eradicate the taboos society has in its attitude toward them. Television and movies have served the homosexual cause well.

Not too many decades ago, Oscar Wilde was prosecuted and jailed for homosexuality, whereas just a few years ago, in the very same England, a noted actor and a famous playright, both professed homosexuals, were knighted by Queen Elizabeth II. Witness the following news release: "The Metropolitan Fellowship of Churches in Miami has tabled a request for membership filed by a local homosexual congregation . . . the action by the fellowship board came after a five-man committee named to study the issue recommended, four to one, that the Metropolitan Community Church be admitted . . . the homosexual congregation, which has about eighty-five members, is part of a denomination which originated in Los Angeles and has branches in twelve to fifteen cities."

Recently, following the ordination of Ellen Barrett, a self-described lesbian, as a deacon in the church, the Rev. Paul Moore, Jr., Episcopal bishop of New York, claimed that it is a sign of healthy change in the attitude toward homosexuality. He made the statement that "historically, many of the finest clergy in our church have had this personality structure . . . homosexuality is a condition which one does not choose; it is not a question of morality."

What of the homosexual and the lesbian? To the physician, homosexuality is a sickness, a deep-rooted psychoneurosis. To the psychiatrist, homosexuality represents a pattern of behavior that is neither inherited nor primarily part of a psychoneurosis, but one that is acquired through learning, association and social forces. The biologist sees a phylogenetic origin for such behavior extending far down the mammalian scale. It is a failure on the part of man to rise above common patterns of sexual activity so frequently observed in lower animals and infrahuman forms. The endocrinologist finds, in general, no remarkable alteration in hormonal levels to characterize the homosexual as different biologically from the norm. Suffice it to say that a biological tendency to inversion of sexual behavior in most, if not all mammals, including Homo sapiens, is strongly suggested by comparative cross-cultural and cross-species studies. Investigators S. C. Ford and F. A. Beach were impressed with the fact that it is the social forces that impinge upon the developing personality from earliest childhood which tend to inhibit and discourage homosexual arousal and behavior and to condition the individual to heterosexual stimuli.

From a survey of the literature it appears that all vertebrates are equipped by nature to perform most of the elementary overt mating patterns of the opposite sex. Experiments have shown that in some animals the copulatory performance of the opposite sex is activated by increasing concentration of the heterologous hormones. This does not mean that the direction of behavior pattern has been changed, since the homologous sex pattern is also simultaneously activated. Although it must not be inferred that sexual aberrations in the human are due to endocrine imbalance, nevertheless, the high incidence of abnormal sexual behavior in men and women with various endocrinopathies cannot be readily dismissed.

In a study by S. J. Glass and R. W. Johnson male sex hormones were administered to eleven male homosexuals; three were improved, five experienced an increase in their homosexual drives. Kinsey felt that there was sufficient clinical experience with the human male to conclude that the intensity of his sexual activity was increased when androgens were administered, whereas his choice of partner (i.e., his heterosexuality or his homosexuality) was not modified. Glass is not entirely in accord with this view, for he believed that a correlation existed between the aggressive, hypersexual homosexual with high androgen production and the passive, hyposexual homosexual with low androgen levels. Glass and his associates believed that the latter type of homosexual could be benefited by androgen therapy insofar as the general somatic inferiority was concerned.

Hormone therapy holds a ray of hope in the management of the lesbian with intensive sex drives. It is generally conceded that although the sex urge in sexual deviants is misdirected, the intensity may be average in most but certainly markedly increased in some. The complete dampening of this sex drive is possible in some females by the administration of progestogens for prolonged periods of time. Revulsion to sexual contact might even set in. In some instances, an opportunity is thus afforded for them to break away and discontinue their homosexual alliances.

The therapeutic approach to the management of homosexuality is indeed a dismal one except for those with endocrinopathies. The clinical curability of selected cases of homosexuality through psychoanalytical treatment is claimed by E. Bergler. On the other hand, W. Steckel, an experienced psychoanalyst, confessed that he had never effected or witnessed a complete cure of homosexuality by analysis. The belief is current that the best psychoanalysis can do is to remove the conscious guilt, thus making the unhappy homosexual a "happy" one.

A detail from Michelangelo's "Creation of Man" in the Sistine Chapel.

31

A Heart of Stone

An eye for an eye . . . a hand for a hand .   Exodus 21:24

Why not a heart for a heart?

THE HUMAN HAND, endowed with a dexterity denied the subhuman form, is the distinguishing accouterment of Homo sapiens. Only humans can approximate the thumb and index finger. The hand has been so necessary an adjunct to human survival that historic man considered loss of the hands the ultimate in punishment.

About 2,000 B.C., the great lawgiver Hammurabi, King of Babylon, laid down certain principles governing remuneration and the legal regulation of medicine. The laws of Hammurabi stated, for instance, "If a physician cause a severe operation wound with a bronze operating knife and cure the patient . . . he shall have ten shekels of silver . . . but if the patient should die, he shall have his hands cut off." Perhaps the disease *furor operativa* was as endemic then as now, and the punishment meted out was severe enough to act as a deterrent to impetuous or reckless surgery.

A thousand years later, this retaliatory concept of justice was incorporated into the Mosaic Code, "Eye for eye, tooth for tooth, hand for hand, foot for foot" (Exodus 21:24) This form of retribution was not extended to medical practice, for the physician was held in the highest esteem and has always enjoyed the respect and confidence of Jewish society. Moreover the law of retaliation, measure for measure, was carried out literally only in capital punishment—a life for a life. Other physical injuries, willful or not, were a matter for monetary and material compensation. The enunciation of this principle is today recognized as one of the most far-reaching steps in human progress. The founders of International Law—Hugo Grotius, Jean Bodin and John Seldin—all maintain that the rule "eye for an eye" enjoins, on the one hand, that a fair and equitable relation exist between the crime and the punishment; and on the other hand, that all citizens are equal before the law appropriate for free peoples. The Mosaic Law was in all probability the beginning of monetary recompense for injury but not for malicious murder: "ye shall take no satisfaction [ransom] for the life of a murderer, which is guilty of death (Numbers 35:31). The literal application of an "eye for an eye" was excluded in Rabbinical Law and there is no instance in Jewish history that this form of retribution was ever executed.

In the benevolent climate of "whatsoever ye would that men should do to you, do you even so to them" (Matthew 7:12) and "what is hateful to thee do it not to another—that is the law, the rest is commentary" (Rabbi Hillel, first century) a compassionate posture toward human frailty and behavior was possible. Turn your other cheek; love your enemies; and forgiveness became the credo of the Western world, although more often honored in the breech than in the observance. Nonetheless, in the best Judeo-Christian tradition, the modern man of medicine has substituted the "hand for a hand" philosophy of Hammurabi with a heart for a heart, a kidney for a kidney. Today, blood vessels are replaced with nylon tubing, a shattered hip with a plastic mold, and perhaps in the near future silastic spheroids slowly oozing testosterone will become available for the man robbed of his birthright by accident of birth or trauma. Teams of cardiac surgeons not only are repairing diseased hearts successfully, but are also desperately trying to replace a failing heart by the transplantation of a healthy one from a dying person.

The mortality rate from heart disease is rising rapidly; it is the second most common cause of death in the industrialized world. Although the first authentic case of coronary thrombosis, diagnosed during life and proved at autopsy, was published by Dr. George Dock in 1886, an account of this disorder can be found in the Old Testament:

And Nabal's heart was merry within him, for he was very drunken: wherefore she told him nothing, less or more, until the morning light. But it came to pass in the morning, when the wine was gone out of Nabal, and his wife had told him these things, that his heart died within him, and he became as a stone. And it came to pass about ten days after, that the Lord smote Nabal, that he died."   1 Samuel 25:36–38

This mean and avaricious sot was guilty of great wrongdoing. His wife, Abigail, tried to make amends and plead for him when his life

190

was threatened by his enemies. When Abigail informed him of the threats, he became enraged and suffered a heart attack. Ten days later, he was dead.

Coronary heart disease seems to have escaped the attention of the medical world for centuries, since it was not until 1768 that the famous British physician, William Heberden, gave a clinical description of a heart attack and its progress from a mild to a fatal illness. He wrote, "There is a disorder of the breast, marked with strong and peculiar symptoms . . . sense of strangling and anxiety with which it is attended may make it not improperly be called angina pectoris." He found that opium afforded relief for this "distemper hitherto unnoticed, that has not yet as far as I know, found a place or a name in the history of diseases."

In 1910, Sir William Osler, during a speech in London, recognized the frame and facies of those prone to heart attacks. He claimed that it was "not the delicate neurotic person . . . but the robust, the vigorous in mind and body, the keen and ambitious man, the indicator of whose engine is always at 'full speed ahead' . . . the well-'set' man from forty-five to fifty-five years of age, with military bearing, iron grey hair, and florid complexion." In fact Osler felt that "the meek shall inherit the earth" because the aggressive achiever often dies prematurely from heart disease. Moreover, he pointed out that angina pectoris tended to show a class distinction, for he asked, "Why is it more common in the upper classes?"

Studies have been initiated to learn the role of social and environmental factors that account for the growing incidence of the disease. Those in the high socioeconomic group are more sensitive to environmental and emotional stress resulting in hormonal changes which effect lipid metabolism (triglycerides, cholesterol, phospholipids). The monkey placed in isolation for seventy-two hours shows an increase in adrenalin and cortisonelike hormones, while testosterone and estrogen levels temporarily fall. Hypothyroid persons, diabetics and ovariectomized women, not on estrogen-replacement therapy, are those most apt to develop coronary heart disease. Coronary heart disease has been shown to be only one-tenth as frequent in women prior to the onset of the menopause than in men before fifty years of age. The difference has been attributed by many investigators to estrogen levels, since the incidence gradually increases as estrogen levels fall in the postmenopausal women, reaching parity with men by sixty-five to seventy years of age.

191

A diet free from or low in animal fat has been advised as a method of lowering cholesterol in the belief that the incidence of coronary heart disease will lessen. Curtis Hames, of Claxton, Georgia, has shown that blacks have a higher saturated fat diet than whites, yet coronary artery disease occurs far less frequently in blacks than in whites, at least in Evans County, Georgia. Because women with normal ovarian function have far less coronary heart disease than men, natural estrogens have been given to men with a history of coronary thrombosis. Dr. Jessie Marmorson of Los Angeles and Dr. Jeremiah Stamler of Chicago have reported that the survival rate in those receiving Premarin, a natural type of estrogen, was significantly higher than in controls. Their data suggested that natural estrogens (but not synthetic) may be antiatherogenic (i.e., may prevent arterio-sclerosis).

Aside from characteristic physical types, ethnic groups, and endo-crine disorders, certain individuals are more prone to myocardial infarction than others: those who cannot control emotional responses; are quick to anger; are given to anxiety, fear, avarice, greed, envy; are mendacious; or those who are overambitious. Kindness, gentleness, tolerance, generosity, and charity are ingredients for prevention of, and balm for, coronary heart disease. From a psychological standpoint, what characterizes the two groups? Osler wrote "that the man who has risen early and late taken rest, who has eaten the bread of carefulness, striving for success in commercial, professional, or politi-cal life is a likely candidate for ischemic heart disease. The habit of working the human machine to its maximum capacity is responsible."

Although surgery is available for certain heart disorders, and the methodology for transplantation of hearts may yet be perfected; and although diets and hormones may prove preventive; nonetheless, the greatest hope for most people lies in a change in emotional makeup and habits and a more amiable everyday philosophy. Jesus' admonition "Take therefore no thought for the morrow: for the morrow shall take thought for the things of itself. Sufficient unto the day is the evil thereof." (Matthew 6:34), may, after, all, be the best medicine. Indeed, the coronary-prone person had been described as one who has a broad time perspective and strong orientation to the future.

Now let us return to Nabal who "became as a stone." It is perhaps coincidental that Shakespeare in *Othello* (Act IV) should use this imagery, "My heart is turn'd to stone." Perhaps the bard "writ better than he knew." Within the past few years, the famous heart-transplant surgeon, Denton A. Cooley, of Houston, Texas, described "stone heart" as a clinical entity—a perplexing phenomenon that occurs during open-heart surgery. The heart is frozen in a state of contracture—a sort of rigor mortis of the heart. The Houston team encountered thirteen fatal cases of stone heart in five thousand open-heart operations.

Organ transplants (heart, lung, liver, kidney and eye) are being tried in ever-increasing numbers. Corneal and kidney transplants have reached a high degree of perfection and are being employed successfully. The transplanting of limbs has been performed experimentally on dogs by Russian scientists. There is a story, somewhat apocryphal, of the man admitted to the hospital with a mangled arm as a result of an accident. He was advised by his surgeon that the arm could not be saved. The distraught man brought to the attention of his physician a newspaper account that had appeared in the Boston press of a young man whose arm was completely evulsed from the shoulder in an automobile crash and how the arm, the nerves, and the blood vessels were successfully reunited to his body. "Why not a human transplant?" he beseeched. The suggestion was taken under advisement and the members of the hospital staff agreed to try, if a proper donor could be found.

Fortunately, or unfortunately, the only arm available belonged to a young woman dying from brain damage caused by a severely fractured skull. The man readily agreed for he felt that a female hand was better than none. The operation was performed. Several months later, he could use his arm well, he wrote with masculine firmness despite the fact that the hand was gentle and delicate. But, when it came to matters of a private and personal nature, the hand fumbled and was reluctant to perform. It seemed, he claimed, that the hand had lost some of its dexterity, but none of its cunning. His use of the words dexterity and cunning reminded me of a little French book *Voici Israel*, in which I found the passage, "Si je t'oublie, O Jerusalem, que ma main droite oublie sa dexterité." Recall that according to the King James version of the Bible, the psalmist sang, "If I forget thee, O Jerusalem, let my right hand forget her cunning" (Psalm 137:5). I have often wondered why there is a difference in terminology—*cunning* versus *dexterity*. This vignette provides an insight into the subtle world of semantics while focusing attention on a new outlook, a new hope for the maimed and diseased—the transplant of limbs, kidneys, eyes and hearts.

193

The Good Samaritan.

194

32

Wine and Penicillin

But a certain Samaritan . . . had compassion on him . . . and bound up his
wounds, pouring in oil and wine.   Luke 11:33, 34

Why wine? Did the ancients believe wine protec-
tive against infection?

WINE AND PENICILLIN seem poles apart; yet, each in its own
sphere is both a boon and a curse. Mankind has benefited from
wine for the pleasure it affords, for its calming influences, and from its
antibiotic properties. Certainly, before science devised a variety of
specifics to ameliorate diverse ailments, wine was an indispensible
boon to mankind. The discoverer of penicillin, Alexander Fleming, in
the last years of his life, was inexorably drawn to the study of wine's
antibiotic properties. Let me unfold for you the saga of wine and
penicillin and show how the two relate; how each has been a
benefactor to mankind while perversely contributing to the depth of
human debauchery and degradation.

The past slowly yields its secrets to the present. When the psalmist
pleaded, "Purge me with hyssop, and I shall be clean" (Psalm 51:77),
he was trying to tell us something. Why hyssop? Was it not employed
a thousand years earlier in the ritual of cleansing the leper and those
afflicted with skin sores of various descriptions? (See Leviticus
14:49-56.) Many years later, Pliny, The Elder (A.D. 23-78), claimed
that the pulverized hyssop leaf, used as a dusting powder, was effective
in cutaneous eruptions and inflammations (Nat. Hist., 20:15,). What is
of particular significance is the fact that the fungus, *Penicillium notatum*,
first identified in 1911 by the Swede, R. Westling, was found growing
on a hyssop plant. The early Egyptians pressed moldy bread to
purulent wounds or swallowed moldy bread for internal maladies, thus
anticipating penicillin and other twentieth century antibiotics from
mold cultures and soil bacteria.

In 1775, by accident, an important discovery was made that grapes, left to rot on the vine, produced a superior wine. This "pourriture noble" is caused by the presence of a special mycoderm. The fungi living as parasites off the pulp of the grape have perhaps rightly earned the sobriquet of "noble rot," because they probably play the decisive role in the acquisition of bactericidal properties by the anthocyanins. It now appears that wine and penicillin are the servants of man because of a common demoninator—the benevolent fungus. Ancient wisdom echoes down through the centuries.

The discovery by Alexander Fleming in 1928 of the antibacterial powers of the mold from which penicillin is derived was sheer serendipity—a triumph of accident and shrewd observation. While he was engaged in research on influenza, mold developed accidentally on a staphylococcus culture plate. He noted that the mold created a bacteria-free circle around itself. Experimenting further, he found that a liquid mold culture, which he named penicillin, prevented growth of staphylococci. He published his work in 1929 in the *British Journal of Experimental Pathology*. This interesting observation was all but ignored. In 1939, pathologist Howard Florey and biochemist Ernst Chain were searching for some substance to control severe infections. Chain was surveying the literature and by sheer luck came across Fleming's paper. He suggested to Florey that they continue where Fleming left off. In 1940, they reported the results of their experiments in *Lancet*; mice injected with a fatal dose of streptococci would survive if treated with penicillin. In 1945, the Nobel Prize was awarded to Fleming, the Scotsman; Florey, the Australian; and Chain, the Jewish refugee from Nazi oppression. Fleming and Florey were knighted by King George VI of England, but Chain was left off the honors list. Years later this honor, long past due, was finally awarded to him.

Before Fleming died in 1955, he became interested in the antibiotic nature of wine. What drew him to this field? Was it because he suspected that fungi, so important to the creation of wine, could account for the well-known antibacterial properties of wine?

Wine was used as an antiseptic in the treatment of wounds for thousands of years. The Good Samaritan, you will recall, when he bound up the wounds of the half-dead traveler, "poured in oil and wine." Hippocrates, Galen, and Dioscorides maintained that there was no better wound dressing than wine. In the Middle Ages, Hugh of Lucca and his son, Theodoric, challenged the doctrine of inducing suppuration ("laudable pus") for the healing of wounds by "secondary intention"; they effected healing with wine alone.

For untold centuries, the prophylactic properties of wine had been suspected. It is recorded that in 539 B.C., Cyrus the Great ordered his armies to carry wine on the march to Babylon as a protection until they could become accustomed to the local drinking water, and thus not fall prey to sickness. The prophylactic measure of adding water to wine has been thought to be a sort of myth, a popular practice handed down from antiquity.

In 1953 the antibiotic action of wine was traced, subsequently, by Jacques Masquelier and his coworkers at the University of Bordeaux to the anthocyanins and related pigments of wine. This bactericidal property is not present in the compound extracted from grapes themselves, but appears only after the fermentation of grapes into wine. In 1960, John J. Powers and his team at the University of Georgia proved that anthocyanin fractions extracted from Pinot Noir wine communicate to wine its bactericidal properties, regardless of the alcohol content. We know today that aqueous solutions of plain alcohol have no effect against most bacilli until the alcohol content is increased to well over thirty per cent, nearly three times the concentration of natural wine. Whereas, Fleming found that penicillin, when diluted eight hundred times, prevented the growth of staphylococci, John Gardner, a pharmacy student, observed that newly fermented wine diluted one hundred thousand times would prove effective.

Wine and alcohol have long been considered aphrodisiacal, either by stimulating sexual desire or by removing one's inhibitions. If wine loosens inhibitions in an unconscious manner, penicillin does so in a conscious way. With the advent of penicillin, many persons who practiced caution for the prevention of venereal infection by utilizing some form of prophylaxis, now throw caution to the winds. Many no longer fear venereal disease, believing that early treatment with penicillin will abort and cure the affliction. The incidence of gonorrhea and syphilis once again approaches epidemic proportions. It may then be said that although wine and penicillin are agents for good, they are also instruments of iniquity. The privileges these agents bring to man are too often abused and the potentials for evil compounded.

Allow me to divert from the main theme by relating the parable of pigeon wisdom. Pigeons flying overhead seldom show disdain for humans. They prefer to defile the belfries of churches and the domes of the halls of justice. A particular passel of pigeons with a proclivity for the window ledge of a certain medical college was subjected to a study in behavioral response. Two bowls, one containing water, the other alcohol, were placed on the ledge where the pigeons came to roost. The carefree birds, after sampling the contents of both bowls, chose to drink water only. When several of the pigeons were trapped and caged, they were again exposed to the same two bowls of liquid. Frustrated, imprisoned, shorn of their freedom, they took to the alcohol, shunning the water. The birds were often seen lying on their backs completely inebriated. So, too, man, when fettered by insecurity, injustice, infidelity, ineptitude, indecision and impotence, often behaves like an incarcerated pigeon. It is written, "Go to the ant, thou sluggard, consider her ways, and be wise" (Proverbs 6:6). And I add— look to the pigeon.

We now can appreciate how benevolent fungi have enabled mankind to enjoy and profit from wine and penicillin.

A vision of the Apocalypse, as described in the book of Revelations.

33

Plants and Drugs of Biblical and Early Times

And there appeared another wonder in heaven; and behold a great red dragon, having seven heads and ten horns, and seven crowns upon his heads.

Revelation 12:3

Was this revelation a psychedelic trip brought on by ingestion of some plant hallucinogen?

HOLY MEN, SEERS, AND PROPHETS attained and maintained their position in tribal society because of the unusual visions they experienced, the voices they heard. Were these wise men privy to the knowledge that the ingestion of certain herbs, plants, or fungi could induce supernatural effects? The revelation of St. John the Divine parallels that of Ezekiel, a prophet of an earlier day, who in the chambers of his imagery saw visions of God.

And I looked, and, behold, a whirlwind came out of the north, a great cloud, and a fire unfolding itself . . .
Also out of the midst thereof came the likeness of four living creatures . . .
And every one had four faces, and every one had four wings. . .
They four had the face of a man, and the face of a lion on the right side; and they four had the face of an ox on the left side; they four also had the face of an eagle.

Ezekiel 1:4-6, 10

In his fascinating book *The Sacred Mushroom and the Cross*, John M. Allegro suggests that hallucinogenic plants, mind-bending mushrooms, and mood-expanding grasses were in common use as part of the cultic practices of prebiblical and biblical times. Did not Isaiah give us some clue to this very possibility and warn that although these plants may bring temporary pleasure, the ultimate rewards are grievous and destructive?

201

Because thou hast forgotten thy God of thy salvation . . . therefore shalt thou plant pleasant plants, and shalt set it with strange slips . . . but the harvest shall be a heap in the day of grief and of desperate sorrow.

Isaiah 17:10

The first savage who nibbled at an herb and found relief from weariness or pain founded the art of pharmacy. Primitive man's constant battle with the elements and his environment, the wild beasts of the field and the hostility of neighboring tribes required that he find calming and healing agents, and that he maintain the right relationship with the omnipotent power that controlled the forces of nature.

The ancestors of man must have been clued in on nature's resources, for they could not fail to observe that animals became wild munching on certain grasses such as the locoweed, and birds often became inebriated while feeding on certain berries. Such observations led to experimentation with plants, herbs, or mineral substances which were endowed with power to heal or kill, and became the subject of study among the witch doctors, priests and prophets of the ancient world. The early doctors were also astrologers, diviners and prognosticators. The art of healing and religion became inextricably entwined. Isaiah warned,

Stand now with thine enchantments and with the multitude of thy sorceries . . . let now the astrologers, the star gazers, the monthly prognosticators, stand up and save thee . . . Behold they shall be as stubble . . . none shall save thee.

Isaiah 12:15

Josephus, the great historian of the first century, said of the Jewish sect called the Essenes that they display "an extraordinary interest in the writing of the ancients, singling out in particular those which make for the welfare of the soul and body; with the help of these, and with a view to the treatment of diseases, they investigate medicinal roots and properties of stones." The cultural successors of these wise men were the Magi of the Gospel account of the birth of Christ (Matthew 2:1) who brought gifts of gold, frankincense and myrrh. They were the original drug peddlers of ancient Persia, Arabia, Ethiopia and Egypt and were the sources of therapeutic folklore. Dioscorides ascribed to the Magi knowledge of the names of drug plants which were called propetai (prophets). Incidentally, the Sumerian word for physician in prebiblical times was prophet, or seer.

Ancient societies usually blamed illness on demons which invaded the body and could be driven out by chants (prayers) and charms, aided by a crude but sometimes effective materia medica which was acquired through trial and error. To these drugs, some of the ancients, such as the Sumerians and the Egyptians, added foul-tasting materials such as insect excreta, cow dung and lizards' eyes, to disgust the demons responsible for the state of health. Egypt's oldest medical records reveal that to soothe a crying child "take pods of the poppy plant and add fly dirt . . . and strain." Paregoric (tincture of opium) is often prescribed by pediatricians for colicky babies. From Babylonian and Assyrian tablets we learn that the heirs of Sumer used belladonna, also known as "deadly nightshade," to poison their enemies. This toxic plant was also used for therapeutic purposes when dissolved and diluted in wine or beer. Unappetizing ingredients usually were added such as bird and bat droppings. Scientists explain the various reactions to this plant by the presence of atropine and scopolamine—standard drugs used today to relax eye muscles, relieve spasms and stimulate the heart.

The ancient Israelites eliminated "the dreck [excreta] pharmacopeia" and employed concoctions of brews, powders, and poultices made from a great variety of mysterious herbs, as well as figs, mustard seed, oils and wines. They also had a keen realization that running water was both preventive and curative—for them "cleanliness was next to godliness." The Jewish ritual of the frequent washing of hands was not understood or appreciated in Christendom. During the Middle Ages, the Jews in the ghettos of Europe often escaped the ravages of the plagues that crisscrossed Europe. The Jews became suspect and were often accused of poisoning the wells. Cleanliness was a disease-preventive, and the importance of the washing of hands was finally brought to light by Ignaz Semmelweis after the middle of the last century. The young Hungarian physician was banished from the hospitals of Vienna for suggesting that obstetricians thoroughly wash their hands before examining a woman in labor. His allegation that childbed fever was spread from one woman to another seemed preposterous to his colleagues. Semmelweis foretold that the alarming death rate from this morbid process could be markedly reduced by so simple a procedure. In time, he was proved right and vindication came years after he was exiled to his native Budapest.

The Holy Land had many plants from which ingredients were

obtained for medicinal and other purposes. The balsam brush was a highly prized shrub. Ezekiel could claim that Judah and Israel had sent to Tyre "honey, oil and balm" and to Dan ". . . cassia and colamus" (27:17). The pistachio bush yielded yellowish white transparent globules, greatly valued for their perfume and healing properties. Other medicinals were galbanum from a parsley-shaped plant (Exodus 30:34), stacte from the storax bush, and onycha from a shrub of the clover family (Exodus 30:34). Hyssop plant was used for cleansing the walls of the leper's house (Leviticus 14:4); and Proverbs 7:17 refers to myrrh, aloes and cinnamon. Incidentally, commercial firms make sunburn lotion from aloe vera. And this same herb which the New Testament says was brought to prepare the body of Christ is now employed to ease external atomic-radiation burns. The people of the Fertile Crescent left a legacy of nature's gifts to medicine in hiero-glyphics, cuneiform, and the written word. In Chapter 3 I made reference to the mandrake root, that alleged aphrodisiac with which Leah purchased a night of connubial bliss with Jacob (Genesis 30:14) and whose narcotic properties could not suffice to give poor Othello "that sweet sleep which thou owedst yesterday."

In a most revealing essay, Lonnelle Aikman wrote glowingly of plant remedies and folk medicine. The great discoveries of drugs resulted from the inquiring and orderly minds of physicians, chemists, botanists and pharmacists who learned through folklore, tribal custom and ancestral rituals, the uses of certain plants, trees, roots, fungi, weeds and flowers for the treatment of physical and mental ailments. For instance, the world's first cure of malaria came from the bark of a flowering evergreen, which was used by the natives to treat fever. The Countess of Chinchón, wife of a seventeenth century viceroy to Peru, brought back to Europe the legends about this tree. Almost two centuries later, pharmaceutical chemists extracted one of the alkaloids from the powdered bark of the cinchona tree and dubbed it quinine, an old Indian term for "bark of barks."

The housewives of rural England knew that a brew of the pretty purple foxglove could relieve dropsy. Dropsy (generalized edema of the body and extremities) occurs in the late stages of heart failure. William Whithering, eighteenth century physician of Birmingham, England, aware of this old wives' tale, labored to extract the active ingredient from the dried leaves of foxglove. Thus, a specific element was discovered, digitalis, which has helped countless millions of heart sufferers.

204

For centuries, Andean Indians used leaves of the coca shrub to escape the harsh realities of their lives. Now we know that the plant's key constituent is cocaine. A young Viennese physician, Sigmund Freud, later to become the founder of psychoanalysis, bought in 1884, a supply of the little known alkaloid from the coca leaf. George Pickering, in his book *Creative Malady*, tells how Freud experimented on himself to learn the physiologic action of the drug. He found that cocaine relieved exhaustion and depression and gave him a sense of exhilaration and euphoria. He also discovered its capacity to anesthetize skin and mucous membrane and so informed his friend Koller, an ophthalmologist. Koller received the credit for demonstrating the local anaesthetic value of cocaine by relieving the excruciating pain attendant upon eye operations. The American surgeon, Halstead, used it for local and regional anaesthesia, becoming addicted to it in the process. Its capacity to produce addiction brought calumny upon Freud's head. Cocaine sniffing has become a fad and a scourge among the pleasure seekers of so-called elite society.

Aztec worshipers revered the mushroom teonanacatl, to escape the bonds of everyday ills. Mescaline from peyote cactus, still a religious tool of the Navajo Indians, sends its users into a euphoric state in which reality seems a distant dream. Psychiatric researchers study these mind-benders, seeking help for the mentally ill. Hashish, the hallucinogenic resin in hemp's flowering tops, called cannabis by botanists, and pot or grass by so-called "moderns" has been used by people of the Middle East for millenia. Doctors of India calmed disturbed patients with rauwolfia, the forerunner of modern tranquilizers. Reserpine derived from rauwolfia, is used to quieten nervous patients and also to reduce high blood pressure.

In the Middle Ages a mysterious plague swept the rye-growing regions of Europe. The victims suffered from hallucinations, convulsions, and burning sensations called St. Anthony's fire. This plague was caused by a fungus blight growing on rye and other grains. In severe cases, constriction of blood vessels occurred, resulting in gangrene of the extremities. Midwives of many lands became aware of the vessel-constricting properties of this purplish fungus growth and made a crude preparation to control bleeding after childbirth. Chemists have isolated ergot from this rye fungus and today, modern doctors prescribe ergot derivatives for postpartum bleeding. In 1951 in Southern France, some of the villagers of St. Esprit, after eating contaminated bread, jumped from windows under the delusion that they could fly—no doubt a bad "LSD" trip. LSD, a man-made drug, is an offshoot of research on ergot alkaloids.

The German apothecary apprentice, Friedrich Sertürner, isolated the first active alkaloid of a natural drug in 1804. The drug was raw opium from the poppy. Sertürner called it morphine after Morpheus, the god of sleep. Morphine is now a mainstay in hospital care for the relief of severe pain and suffering. Sertürner's pioneer work started a chemical revolution, and chemists have continually tried since that time to isolate and synthesize drugs from nature's vegetation.

Consider the willow tree. For centuries, willow bark and leaves yielded resins and juices to ease aches and pains of rheumatism and neuralgia. The rural folk of the mountains of Virginia and the Carolinas have treated fevers with a decoction of willow bark. The active ingredient in such remedies was revealed in 1820 as salicin, named for the willow genus, Salex. In 1899, a related synthetic product, acetyl salicylic acid, called aspirin, was introduced. Aspirin has become a household word—the most popular and perhaps the most generally useful medicament in the world.

In primitive societies, medicine became entwined with religion. Evil spirits were blamed for human ills and witch doctors often took hallucinogens in the hope of contacting the outer world, or gave them to the afflicted in an effort to bring relief.

For over forty centuries, civilizations amassed a wealth of knowledge about plants for medicinal use. The Greek physician, Hippocrates, set the stage for the world's turn from incantations and charms to practical medicine. The early Greeks obtained from the autumn crocus a drug called colchicum that has been used for over two thousand years for the treatment of gout. Maimonides, twelfth century Jewish physician, refers to it in his *Aphorisms*. In 1974, a new use was found for this drug—the successful management of Mediterranean fever, a hitherto mysterious and incurable disease.

In every culture and in every age, man has looked to the plant world to cure his ills. And in the same plant world he has found ingredients to help him forget his troubles, ease his pain and lift his depression. Certain drug plants often caused him to hallucinate, to dream dreams and to see visions. The life and letters of the poet Samuel Taylor Coleridge (1772-1834) epitomize the influence of opium on his lifestyle. His poetic flights of fancy brought him to distant and enchanting lands.

> In Xanadu did Kubla Khan
>> A stately pleasure-dome decree. . .
> It was a miracle of rare device,
> A sunny pleasure-dome with caves of ice!

He finally captures the very essence of his euphoric escapade when he explains that "Kubla heard from afar ancestral voices prophesying" and concludes his masterful poem with:

> His flashing eyes, his floating hair!
> Weave a circle round him thrice,
> And close your eyes with holy dread,
> For he on honey-dew hath fed,
> And drunk the milk of Paradise.

Coleridge ended his days as a recluse and a broken man. Isaiah had indeed admonished that the planting of "pleasant" plants would ultimately bring grief and despair. Note Coleridge's choice of such words in his metaphors as "miracle," "prophesying," "holy," "paradise." For me, they conjure up images of the holy men of a distant past, whose religious experiences may well have been induced by mind-expanding herbs.

Jesus giving sight to the man blind from birth.

34

The Sins of the Fathers

As Jesus passed by, he saw a man which was blind from his birth. And his disciples asked him, saying, Master, who did sin, this man or his parents, that he was born blind? Jesus answered, Neither hath this man sinned, nor his parents.   John 9:2-3

Is heritable disease a sequel to sin?

E ARLY IN THE HISTORY of the Jews, sickness was equated with sin. This attitude toward disease was carried over into the New Testament for there, too, reference is made to sin's being responsible for illness. "Behold thou art made whole: sin no more, lest a worse thing come unto thee" (John 5:14). The Decalogue expressly states, "I the Lord thy God am a jealous God, visiting the iniquity of the fathers upon the children unto the third and fourth generation" (Exodus 20:5). Biblical scholars and theologians interpret the Second Commandment as an exhortation not to break the Ten Commandments. As a deterrent, a threat looms that illness will be passed from one generation to the next. Such sentiments were also held by the ancient Greeks centuries before the birth of Christ for Euripides (484-406 B.C.) wrote, "The Gods visit the sins of the fathers upon the children." Many students of the Talmud (the ancient commentary of the Old Testament) do not feel that the sins of the guilty fathers should be visited upon innocent children. Yet, the Bible furnishes the example of King David who sinned, and as a result, "The Lord struck the child . . . and it was very sick" (2 Samuel 12:15). And there is the story of the widow whose son was so sick that,

There was no breath left in him. And she said unto Elijah, "What have I to do with thee, O thou man of God? art thou come unto me to call my sin to remembrance, and to slay my son?"   1 Kings 17:18

Recall that the Bible here records the first use of mouth-to-mouth resuscitation; thus did Elijah revive the child.

Illness was considered to be an expression of God's wrath as a result of sins committed by fathers, or mothers, or their forebears.

> Our fathers have sinned . . . and we have borne their iniquities.
>
> Lamentations 5:7

In his book, *Medicine in the Bible*, Charles J. Brim saw in such a passage a reminder that adultery, fornication and perversion led to venereal disease and that congenital syphilis was often one of the ill-rewards of such transgressions. The English physician, Hutchinson, described widely spaced, notched teeth as a stigma of congenital syphilis. According to Brim, Jeremiah's warning, "The children's teeth are set on edge" (Jeremiah 31:29) probably meant "Hutchinson's teeth." The presence of gonorrhea in a parturient woman may cause eye infection in the newborn often leading to blindness. Thus, we have at least two examples of the sins of the fathers (and mothers, too) affecting the next generation. Congenital disorders are present at birth and are not to be confused with hereditary genetic disorders which are transmitted for many generations.

Heritable diseases are believed to be far more common in societies in which first-cousin marriages are frequent. The presumption of consanguinity is strong among tight-knit ethnic groups such as the Jews. Ezekiel, in writing about the death of his wife, for whom he was not to indulge in the usual mourning rites, may have described a hereditary disorder (24:16). This reference was picked up some twenty-five centuries later by Dr. C. Riley of New York who called it "familial dysautonomia." Two cardinal symptoms characterize this syndrome—an inability to produce tears, and a decreased sensitivity to pain. Among other features are behavioral problems, corneal anaesthesia with ulceration, poor speech and odd gait. Dr. Simon S. Levin, in his remarkable book *Adam's Rib*, offers the following explanation:

> Son of man, (hereditary influence) behold, I take away from thee the desire of thine eye (corneal anaesthesia with ulceration) with a stroke: (pathology in the central nervous system) yet neither shalt thou mourn (incongruous behavioral response) nor weep (insensitivity to pain), neither shall thy tears run down (failure of lacrimation). Ezekiel 24:16.

Genetically transmitted disease has become an important aspect of medicine. Geneticists are attracted to the fact that a difference in heritable disease occurs in the two main branches of Jewry—the Ashkenazi (Germanic) and the Sephardi (Spanish). The disorders—Gaucher, Tay-Sachs, Hand-Schuller-Christian, all the result of an accumulation of abnormal lipid (fat) substances in different organs—are 30 to 40 times more common among Ashkenazi than among all other populations of the world. On the other hand, familial Mediterranean fever, characterized by recurrent bouts of fever and acute attacks of abdominal pain, is found almost exclusively among Sephardi but has also been noted among Armenians and Arabs. It is extremely rare among all other races. No form of therapy availed until very recently when it was found that Colchicum (from which colchicine is obtained), a drug in use for a thousand years can banish the symptoms.

The discovery that Ashkenazi and Sephardi distinguish themselves not only culturally but also by their hereditary disorders has excited Professor J. J. Groen of the Hebrew University-Hadassah Hospital. He reasoned that the answer might lie in the historic separation of these two groups. The Israelites were divided into twelve tribes, each given a territory of its own in the Holy Land. They were united under King David but separated after the death of King Solomon. The tribes of Judah and Benjamin formed the southern kingdom, Judeah or Judea; the remaining ten tribes comprised the northern kingdom, Israel. In 586 B.C. Judea was invaded by the forces of Nebuchadnezzar and most of the inhabitants were carried off to Babylon. Fifty years later Cyrus the Great, of Persia, set them free and they returned almost en masse to Jerusalem and Judea where they lived for the next six hundred years. The revolt of the Jews against the Romans (A.D. 66-70) resulted in their ultimate subjugation and the destruction of the Temple. Seventy thousand Judeans were taken captive and exiled to Rome. The Arch of Titus bearing the words "Judea Capta" stands majestically in the center of Rome commemorating the victory. After their servitude (the construction of the vast Colosseum), a migration began to countries under Roman rule. Later, the tolerance of Charlemagne (Charles der Grosse) permitted their dispersion throughout the Holy Roman Empire. Jews lived along the Rhine for a thousand years before the rampaging Crusaders and systematic persecution disturbed their lives. Again, the Jews were on the move and they settled in more hospitable lands of Western, Central and Eastern Europe. Communication with one another regardless of where they lived was through a common folk language—their Germanic jargon of former days—which became known as Yiddish. These are the Ashkenazi.

What about the Sephardic Jews? What of their origins? About one hundred and thirty-six years before the conquest of Judea by the Babylonians, the Kingdom of Israel was overrun by the Assyrians and other hostile neighbors. The ten tribes were scattered; many were taken captive, others were lost. In time, according to Philip Gillon of the *Jerusalem Post*, the remnants of the Lost Tribes found refuge in the many lands of the Middle East, Asia Minor, Egypt and North Africa. Great numbers of their descendants followed the conquering Moors into Spain. There for the next five centuries, they prospered and contributed greatly to the culture, material wealth and glory of the country as scholars, physicians, merchants and financiers. The advent of the fifteenth century, however, did not augur well for them, and conversion to Christianity became a modus vivendi for many aspiring Jews in order to circumvent the growing discrimination and obstructions to their progress.

Queen Isabella, influenced by Bishop Torquemado, decided to rid Spain of heretical forces. Conversion to Catholicism or banishment was the decree. About the time Columbus was ready to sail on his voyage of discovery in 1492, the infamous Inquisition was set up to flush out heretics and to torture those who professed Catholicism but practiced their religion in secret (the Marranos). Fragmentary information appears from time to time to suggest that Columbus' parents were Marranos who left Spain for Genoa, Italy in all probability to escape suspicion and persecution. Simon Wiesenthal, in *Sails of Hope*, writes that "Columbus had an excellent library, was exceedingly well-educated for a person of rather humble beginnings, had a knowledge of Hebrew and used a secret Hebrew cipher when writing his son Diego, and he was especially well-versed in the Old Testament. He was also an excellent cartographer, a trade practiced almost entirely by Jews." The expenses of the Columbus expedition were met, not as the romantic story has it, by the pawning of Queen Isabella's crown jewels, but by treasures confiscated from Jewish property. The Marrano financier—Luis de Santangel—furnished 17,000 florins to equip the expedition. Jewish geographers and astronomers, notably Abraham Zacuto, rendered Columbus immense service. Several men of Jewish origin were among his crew, along with the interpreter and some key personnel. Although about 200,000 Jews left Spain, many thousands did convert and became "New Christians." The late Generalissimo Francisco Franco, Chief of the Spanish State, and his wife were of this breed. Professor Dos Santos of Lisbon, Portugal (his father was the discoverer of aortography—the method of outlining organs by injection of radiolucent dyes into the main conduit of arterial blood, the aorta), told me of his antecedents and that his ancestors became New Christians after the Inquisition came to Portugal. Portugal lost her cartographers, and without these skilled mapmakers the Portuguese navigators lost their preeminence on the seas. Delftware, known throughout the world, owes its fame to the Delft family who fled Portugal for Holland taking with them their knowledge of ceramics.

The Inquisition forced most of the Jews of Spain and Portugal to migrate to North Africa, Salonica, Venice, Italy, Bulgaria, Turkey, Egypt, the Island of Rhodes and Southern France; a small number went to Holland (the Spinosas) and later to England (the Disraelis), to South America and the West Indies. It is of some interest to know that the first boatload of Sephardi arrived in New Amsterdam (now Manhattan) in 1654 from Brazil because of the ubiquitous Inquisition. The Sephardi, no matter what country they inhabited, maintain even to this day, their particular language of communication, a Spanish jargon known as Ladino. In the United States, two great jurists of the Supreme Court are exemplars of the two groups. Justice Benjamin Cardozo, idealist and humanitarian, was of Sephardic origin. Justice Felix Frankfurter, pragmatist, and ebullient, innovative interpreter of the United States Constitution, is of Ashkenazi stock. Until recently the two groups remained more or less separate, marrying amongst themselves.

Genetic diseases are primarily chromosomally determined. Of the complement of forty-six chromosomes present in every cell of the body, two are sex chromosomes, the rest are autosomes. Genetic diseases, both sex-linked and autosomal, are more prominent in those societies in whom inbreeding is common. Hemophilia, a blood disease, is frequent in the inbred royal families of Europe. Mediterranean anemia (thalassemia) is found in persons of Mediterranean and Southeast Asian Origin. Phenylketonuria (PKU) manifests itself by severe mental retardation. It is an inborn error of metabolism involving one of the amino acids and is found most often in people of North Irish and West Scottish stock. Porphyria is another heritable biochemical disturbance with a variety of clinical manifestations such as skin eruptions and nervous system disorders. A diagnostic finding is the turning of a urine specimen to a burgundy red color on exposure to sunlight. The Georgian kings of England are said to have suffered from this chemical aberration. King George III (1738-1820), during whose reign the American colonies gained their independence, suffered many bouts of insanity. The last few years of his life were spent in seclusion; he was blind as well as mad. Sickle-cell anemia, which presents as anemia with recurrent pain in extremities and abdomen, is observed almost exclusively in American blacks. Diabetes and idiopathic hirsutism, each in itself a familial disorder, occur mainly in Caucasians of European extraction. This syndrome, a double ancestral curse, was described by Achard and Thiers as "la femme diabète à barbe."

During my training in pathology in 1933 at one of Boston's hospitals, I was in a position to assist in the diagnosis of a mysterious malady that afflicted the brother of a friend. The liver biopsy revealed the fat-laden cells peculiar to Gaucher's disease. I informed my friend, a deacon of a church, that I was puzzled by the findings, since the disease occurred mainly in Jews. He appeared somewhat embarrassed and muttered that his mother was partly Jewish. He did not know as I did that an autosomal recessive trait is handed down only when both mother and father are carriers of a particular gene even though the chance of having an affected child is but one in four. I do hope that denial of one's heritage is not a sin and that the children will not suffer because of the iniquity of the father.

The categorization of dozens of hereditary diseases and the clarification of the role of genes and chromosomes in hereditary disease has been one of the highlights of medicine in the past decade. When sickness and sin were synonyms, the author of Lamentations could indeed cry, "Our fathers have sinned . . . and we have borne their iniquities." Neither disease nor nonconformity to religious ritual are denominators of evil. My late mentor, Dr. Lombard G. Kelly, President of the Medical College of Georgia, related to me that the pastor of his church warned that a newborn child not baptized by immersion in running water was doomed to everlasting hell. Dr. Kelly walked out of the church never to return. For the innocent to suffer was as abhorrent to him as it is to present-day Judeo-Christian thought. Sin may indeed bring on anguish, a guilt-ridden conscience, and illness but to believe that such sickness may be visited upon the children to the third and fourth generation surely is not in harmony with present-day medical knowledge.

Despite plague, pestilence, persecution, heritable diseases and repeated attempts at genocide, the mystique of Jewish survival astounds the world. Rome fell 1,500 years ago, and the once proud and surging Spanish Empire has dwindled to but a shell of its former power. It is ironic to learn that in the First Century A.D., Pliny the Younger, as governor of the Roman province of Bithynia, wrote to Emperor Trajan that those subjects caught or reported practicing Christianity in secrecy were severely punished or executed. Such deterrents however, he claimed did not stem the crime but seemed to stimulate the spread of this deception. The Emperor, with civility and humaneness replied:

"The Christians are not to be sought out; if reported and convicted, they are to be punished, with this reservation . . . however suspect he may have been in the past, shall obtain pardon by penitence. Anonymous publications ought to have no place in a criminal charge. It is a thing of the worst example and unworthy of our age."

Queen Isabella learned nothing from history and permitted Bishop Torquemado to continue his tortures and the auto-da-fé spectacles (burning of heretics) of those new Christians who were suspected of practicing Judaism in secret. The early Jewish Christians, spread throughout the Roman Empire suffered a similar fate fourteen centuries earlier.

The more things change, the more they remain the same. Some unknown poet wrote,

> How odd of God
> To choose the Jews
> But odder still
> To choose a Jewish God . . .

List of Illustrations and Acknowledgements

Acknowledgement is hereby made for kind permission to use the following illustrations.

218

Index of Names